Palgrave Macmillan Studies in Family and Intimate Life

Series Editors
Lynn Jamieson
University of Edinburgh
Edinburgh, UK

Jacqui Gabb
Faculty of Arts & Social Sciences
Open University
Milton Keynes, UK

Sara Eldén
Lund University
Lund, Sweden

Chiara Bertone
University of Eastern Piedmont
Alessandria, Italy

Vida Česnuitytė
Mykolas Romeris University
Vilnius, Lithuania

'The Palgrave Macmillan Studies in Family and Intimate Life series is impressive and contemporary in its themes and approaches'
– Professor Deborah Chambers, Newcastle University, UK, and author of *New Social Ties*.

The remit of the Palgrave Macmillan Studies in Family and Intimate Life series is to publish major texts, monographs and edited collections focusing broadly on the sociological exploration of intimate relationships and family life. The series encourages robust theoretical and methodologically diverse approaches. Publications cover a wide range of topics, spanning micro, meso and macro analyses, to investigate the ways that people live, love and care in diverse contexts. The series includes works by early career scholars and leading internationally acknowledged figures in the field while featuring influential and prize-winning research.

This series was originally edited by David H.J. Morgan and Graham Allan.

Getrude Dadirai Gwenzi

Rethinking the Meaning of Family for Adolescents and Youth in Zimbabwe's Child Welfare Institutions

palgrave
macmillan

Getrude Dadirai Gwenzi
University of Johannesburg
Johannesburg, South Africa

ISSN 2731-6440   ISSN 2731-6459   (electronic)
Palgrave Macmillan Studies in Family and Intimate Life
ISBN 978-3-031-23374-6   ISBN 978-3-031-23375-3   (eBook)
https://doi.org/10.1007/978-3-031-23375-3

This Palgrave Macmillan imprint is published by the registered company Springer Nature Switzerland AG.
The registered company address is: Gewerbestrasse 11, 6330 Cham, Switzerland

I dedicate this book to my family, you are a blessing to me.

PREFACE

This book is inspired by my professional and personal background, which is guided by my passion for the lives of children in care and care leavers globally and in Zimbabwe. In the context of Zimbabwe and much of Southern Africa, not much is known about the lives of children and young people who grow up in child welfare institutions, and they are often marginalised in mainstream discourse. In general, care-experienced youths are a marginalised group in Zimbabwe. I was fortunate to be introduced to the lives of children and young people without parental care during my first job as a social worker in 2009. For several years, I worked in the Child Protection sector in Cape Town, South Africa, before I decided to pursue further studies that have helped me to better understand their plight. The ideas presented in this book emanate from my doctoral thesis, which was awarded by Lingnan University, Hong Kong, in November 2019.

In this book, I wanted not only to contribute to the dearth of literature on family meanings in Zimbabwe but also to understand family meanings as they apply to vulnerable youth groups, such as those living in child welfare institutions. The child welfare institution is a nonnormative living arrangement for orphans and vulnerable children (OVCs), and despite the many studies that have been conducted on their lives, there is no specific focus on the family lives of youths living in this setting. There is a general lack of book publications on family in Zimbabwe and a lack of studies on the meanings ascribed to the term "family" by children and young people growing up separately from their biological families. We often take it for granted that every child grows up in a family environment, and the lives of those who grow up in out-of-home care or without parental care have been marginalised both in research and public discourse. This book is therefore concerned with understanding how OVCs living in child welfare institutions make sense of "family", which is a critical component in their lives.

Conceptually, my thinking originated from my social work background with looked-after children, and I applied sociological principles of "family" that allowed me to explore broader meanings of "family" that would make sense for youths living in nonnormative settings. My doctoral project applied sociological concepts of "family" to a largely social work issue, that of alternative care for children separated from their birth families. The multiple relationships with social workers, caregivers and other individuals who children and youths are exposed to in the child welfare system and the strained relationships with their birth families led me to question the narrow definition of "family" that only considers blood or biological ties as legitimate family. In my social work practice, I also observed that youths would be reunified with their birth families, that these placements would fail, and that youths would return to the child welfare institution seeking help. I concluded that these failed placements could have been avoided if practitioners had considered what family actually means for these young people. The young people I worked with during my years as a social worker often relied on friends, church members and community well-wishers, more than their blood relations for support and as their close relations. I then sought to study whether these close relations could be considered "family" or, if not, how adolescents and youths in child welfare institutions even defined family and who was family for them.

Owing to my background as a child protection social worker and an early career researcher who has focused on the alternative care of children, I consider the benefits of adopting a broader understanding of families that encompass all groups of individuals, including those growing up in nonnormative living environments. It goes without saying that children with care experience will become adults who will be reintegrated back into families and communities. Their experience of separation and placement in institutional care is therefore viewed as temporary. Similar to young people without a care history, adolescents and young people in institutions go through emerging adulthood, which is described as the age of identity explorations, the age of instability, the self-focused age, the age of feeling in-between and the age of possibilities (Arnett, 2010). Family formations are also part of this exploration phase. Therefore, knowledge of how youths construct family meanings not only is useful for society at large but will also help social service practitioners and policymakers who plan interventions to support youth transitions at various stages, including the emerging adulthood stage.

Johannesburg, South Africa   Getrude Dadirai Gwenzi

REFERENCES

Arnett, J., Adolescence, J., & Adulthood, E. (2010). *A Cultural Approach*. Prentice Hall.

Acknowledgements

First and foremost, I give thanks to the Most High God, the Almighty who is the source of my strength and inspiration for all that I do. A special thanks to my doctoral supervisors, Professor Annie Chan Hau-Nung and Professor Roman David in the Department of Sociology and Social Policy at Lingnan University, who guided and supervised the study on which this book is based. Their guidance and supervision allowed me to see the questions in this book in a broader light and convinced me of the significance of this topic not only for social work and the sociology of family but also for broader society. I also want to express my gratitude to my Lingnan Africa community, who helped me through my doctoral journey in Hong Kong and provided me with a community. Special mention goes to Dr Uchechi Shirley Anaduaka, my confidant, friend and sister from another mother. You gave me the strength to go on when times were tough and always taught me to believe in something greater than me. To my friend, Dr Michael Addaney, thank you for giving me the opening introduction that started the process of me writing this book. Thank you for your expert guidance and gentle advice. To my family and friends, for bearing with me during the gruelling months when I had to write and think through the ideas in this book. Thank you for your patience. Ashby Hanyire, thank you for believing in me and encouraging me. Last, but definitely not least, I would like to express my sincere gratitude to the adolescents and youths who participated in this study. Your voices allowed the ideas in this book to come to life because of your life experiences and the family memories that you shared with me. I am forever grateful to you for allowing me to enter your lives in this way, and I sincerely hope that I have done justice to your narratives in this book.

CONTENTS

ABBREVIATIONS

BEAM	Basic Education Assistance Module
CHHs	Child-headed households
CRNSA	Child Rights Network for Southern Africa
CWPC	Children Without Parental Care
DSS	Department of Social Services
DSW	Department of Social Welfare
ESAP	Economic Structural Adjustment Program
GCE	General Certificate of Education
HIV/AIDS	Human immunodeficiency virus/Acquired Immunodeficiency syndrome
ISC	Interpretive Social Constructionism
MPLSW	Ministry of Public Service, Labour and Social Welfare
OOHC	Out-of-home care
OSC	Orphaned and separated children
OVCs	Orphans and Vulnerable Children
RCCF	Residential Child Care facility
UNGA	United Nations General Assembly
UNICEF	United Nations Children's Fund

LIST OF FIGURES

LIST OF TABLES

CHAPTER 1

Introduction

Everything in life is connected, and everything is connected to family
—Lemn Sissay (*2016*).

For centuries, the notion of family has been taken for granted, with everyone holding similar assumptions about its structure and definition. There is also the prevailing belief that everyone experiences family in the same way, which is not necessarily based on reality. The traditional standard definition of the family painted the idea of coresidency, with two heterosexual parents living with their child(ren), the family being kept together by long-lasting, reciprocal bonds of love, support and loyalty. This idealistic notion of family has persisted for several generations, and according to the Organisation for Economic Co-operation and Development (OECD, 2011), changes in families have only started gaining recognition in the last 30 or so years. Furstenberg (2014) explains the several changes we have seen in families as a result of the adaptation of individuals to changing economic, demographic, technological and cultural conditions. Consequently, several studies have been conducted to explain and document family changes in the last few decades, highlighting the increasing diversity of family structures, relationships and meanings. (e.g., Bigombe, & Khadiagala, 2004; Heath, 2012; Shen et al., 2021).

© The Author(s), under exclusive license to Springer Nature Switzerland AG 2023
G. D. Gwenzi, *Rethinking the Meaning of Family for Adolescents and Youth in Zimbabwe's Child Welfare Institutions*, Palgrave Macmillan Studies in Family and Intimate Life,
https://doi.org/10.1007/978-3-031-23375-3_1

Different forms of family emerged in the last few decades, including blended, same-sex, adoptive and foster families. All these different forms of family have been vying for their place in society and claiming their legitimacy. Several reasons have been proposed to explain the changes in family relationships, which encompass the inclusion of women in the workplace; women's increased educational and career opportunities; the introduction of contraceptives; Lesbian, Gay, Bisexual, Transgender and Queer (LGBTQ) movements; increased involvement of fathers in the lives of their children; and the advent of assisted reproductive technologies that have altered conception methods. With regard to the latter, babies born through artificial insemination have raised questions about their social and emotional well-being, and there have been debates about the legitimacy of surrogate families (e.g., Golombok & Tasker, 2015). Different family types have since emerged, and there have been debates about their legitimacy, especially when compared to the traditional nuclear family ideal. For instance, children raised in nontraditional families, such as single-parent families, have been documented to have negative outcomes compared to children in families with both parents (e.g., Ribar, 2015).

The complexity of families has only just increased in the face of this diversity and multiplicity of meanings of what can be a "family". Particularly in the developing world, narrow definitions that only focus on consanguinity and biolegal relationships are no longer as dominant as they were 30 or so years ago. Contemporary perspectives on family within sociology have argued that other concepts, such as togetherness, closeness and belongingness, can be bases for constructing family meanings for individuals (Cutas & Chan, 2012; Ribbens-McCarthy, 2012). In other words, individuals can now describe individuals as "family" based on the fact that their perception of the connection between them and these bonds may form due to proximity, shared experiences and resources.

This book addresses the meaning of family in two ways: what is family (*family definition*) and who counts as family (*family membership*). The perspectives presented in the study are those of adolescents and youths living in child welfare institutions in Zimbabwe, a developing country in the southern part of Africa. It may be surprising for some to understand the focus on family meanings for young people growing up outside of biological family care. You may be asking, why study family young people without "family". Throughout this book, I will highlight how family remains a very pertinent aspect even during separation. It may take a different form and meaning, but it remains present in the lives of adolescents and youths living outside of biological family care. In Zimbabwe and most of sub-Saharan Africa, children and young people who grow up in child welfare institutions and other forms of substitute care, also known as care-experienced youths (MacDonald et al., 2020; Quarmby et al., 2019), are a marginalised group who have not been included in social policies until recently. The Children's Act (Chapter 5:06) provides guidelines for the care of children up to the age of 18 and makes no provisions for those who leave care as adults. The National Orphan Care Policy of 1999 also mentions children who end up in residential child care facilities. However, there is a dearth of information on their family relationships and how they construct the meaning of family.

Youths living with nonparental caregivers experience at least one family transition, which indicates instability and can have a negative impact on youths (Vandivere et al., 2012). Many of them may have no homes to return to upon leaving care and often have a history of unstable living arrangements, including multiple placements and time spent living on the streets (Briggs et al., 2012). Most care leavers in Zimbabwe struggle to reintegrate into society and face several social challenges (Gwenzi & Ringson, 2023; Gwenzi, 2019). Compared to adolescents and youths living with and growing up in their families, those in child welfare institutions may have difficulties making sense of their family relationships (Gwenzi, 2020). They may struggle to trust people due to their traumatic pasts, which affects their ability to form meaningful connections even as adults (Bengtsson & Mølholt, 2018; Butterworth et al., 2017).

In this book, I use the phrase "adolescents and youths" to describe young people living in child welfare institutions. The term "youth" varies between countries based on the sociocultural, institutional, economic and political factors in each country (Efem, 2007). As such, it is socially constructed (Espejo, 2015). In general, youth has been defined as a phase of life between childhood and adulthood. For statistical purposes, the United Nations (UN, 2008) defines youth as persons aged between 15 and 24 years of age. In Zimbabwe, youths are defined as persons between the ages of 15 and 35 (National Youth Policy, 2013). The age group 13–17 was chosen to prevent challenges that come with conducting research with much younger children in institutions. This group includes a group of adolescents who do not fall in the category of youths based on the definitions above. The phrase "adolescents and youths" will be used interchangeably with young people throughout the book.

This book contributes to the growing ideological shift in the study of families and personal relationships. In Zimbabwe, not much is known about how young people make sense of their family relationships, despite the many changes that have taken place in Zimbabwean families. The growing diversity of families in Zimbabwe has been caused by globalisation and modernisation, and the dearth of studies on this topic is concerning. More importantly, the book focuses on a nonnormative group of adolescents and youths living outside of family care. The subject of family as it pertains to separated young people living in child welfare institutions is a neglected area of scholarship both within sociology and social work disciplines. The main presumption (hypothesis) in this book is that the experience of being separated from the biological family and placed in a child welfare institution will influence adolescents' and youths' constructions of "family" by definition and membership. This is because young people living in child welfare institutions often hail from backgrounds in which they experience adverse childhood circumstances, including abuse, neglect, maltreatment and loss, all of which may distort their family views. The experience of being separated from the biological family also contributes to shaping their views on family. This book will show how the separation experience coupled with life in the child welfare institution influences the social construction of family meanings by adolescents and youths in Zimbabwe.

The unique stance that was taken when writing this book challenges contemporary sociological analyses of "family", which have largely ignored nonnormative living environments for children, such as residential care by non-kin caregivers. Child welfare institutions are increasingly occupied by millions of young people globally (Lumos, 2017). According to Csáky (2009), eight million of the world's children grow up in institutions. Due to the pervasive nature of families in our society, this neglect of marginalised groups' views on families will leave us with an incomplete picture of how families are progressing in our societies or how they are being understood by the wider society. In particular, the book argues for the inclusion of the voices of marginalised young people from disadvantaged backgrounds, including a history of family separation. The views of adolescents and youths in child welfare institutions in this book are juxtaposed with the views of orphans and vulnerable children (OVCs) living in their birth families. This comparison allowed for a deeper analysis that highlighted the similarities between children who grow up with their families and those who grow up outside family care in Zimbabwe. The nuances that exist in the understanding of family meanings were brought out more clearly when young people in institutions were compared with those in families.

THE SOCIAL EXCLUSION OF YOUTHS IN INSTITUTIONS

To further elucidate the social exclusion and marginalisation of institutionalised youths, this section provides support for the critical social work argument above. The definition of social exclusion adopted in this book is by Pierson (2010, p. 12):

> *a process [over time] that deprives individuals and families, groups and neighbourhoods of the resources required for participation in the social, economic and political activity of society as a whole. This process is primarily a consequence of poverty and low income, but other factors, such as discrimination, low educational attainment and depleted living environments, also underpin it. Through this process, people are cut off for a significant period in their lives from institutions and services, social networks and developmental opportunities that the great majority of a society enjoys.*

This definition addresses the critical reason why most young people end up being separated from their birth families and in institutions, especially in the context of developing countries such as Zimbabwe—poverty. Poverty is the root of social exclusion according to the above definition. This social exclusion continues as young people become adults, especially if the reasons why they were separated are not properly dealt with while they are in care. When youths leave state care (including institutional or residential care), they experience poor outcomes in employment and education (Furey & Harris-Evans, 2021; McNamara et al., 2019).

In most cases, child welfare institutions are separated from the rest of the community, with minimal interaction of children with the outside community being justified as child protection. Although children in institutions might meet other children living with their families at school, church or other community organisations, their lived experiences will always differentiate them. The extrafamilial group life in the child welfare institution exposes adolescents and youths to a different kind of upbringing and a different socialisation compared to their peers living in families in the community.

Institutional care varies from one institution to another in a given country and from one country to another, and there may be differences within a single country (McCall & Groark, 2015). Each institution or group home has its own culture (Anglin, 2002). The aims of institutional care may also vary between countries. In general, the ethos of institutional shelters is to provide the child and adolescent with reception, care and a space for socialisation and development, offering the possibility of a positive and stable relationship with a caregiver (de Jesus Fontel Cunha Donato et al., 2017, p. 1162). In Europe, institutional care, defined as residential health or social care facilities with 11 or more children, where children stay for more than three months without a primary caregiver (Browne, et al., 2006), was reportedly used mostly for young children in need (either because their biological parents have died or abandoned them or because their parents do not have the means to care for them appropriately). In South Asia, there is an over-persistence on the use of institutional care, and they are mostly run by non-governmental organisations (de Silva, 2007).

This is similar to most countries in sub-Saharan Africa. In 2015, Africa was home to approximately 55 million orphans (Embleton et al., 2014), and currently, the continent has approximately 32.1 million orphaned children (Children International, 2022). Most orphans end up in institutional forms of alternative care.

There are, however, certain features of institutional care that are common across countries and continents, including generally high child-to-caregiver ratios, lowly paid caregivers with little education or training who work rotating shifts, regimented and nonindividualised care, and a lack of psychological investment in the children (Dozier, et al., 2012). Furthermore, scholars have questioned whether residential care settings can be considered as "home" by residents, including children (see e.g., Börjesson, & Torgé, 2022; Clark et al., 2015; Dorrer et al., 2010) and what factors may contribute to making it more like home, especially for children and young people who need more than just temporary care. Extrafamilial group living, in most cases, has been found to be lacking in terms of being a place where children can call "home". Anglin (2002) argues that no matter how much a group home comes as close to a family as possible and creates a sense of family life, the young people living in those settings are always aware that it is not "normal" for them to grow up there.

The temporal nature of care also deters institutionalised young people from feeling completely "at home" and forming lasting relationships with individuals in this setting. The separation from the community may also mean that young people have less access to cultural training and social skills that are present in mainstream society. Without adequate knowledge of the local culture and social skills, youths in Ghana were found to struggle to re-establish ties with family members, which in turn led to stigma and rejection in different life domains (Frimpong-Manso, 2018). Studies in Zimbabwe have noted the detrimental effects of the old model of institutional care, dormitory-style institutions, and how the government of Zimbabwe has moved away from this model to a family-style model that was said to be more accommodating of indigenous value systems of family living and community. The conditions that necessitate the need for alternative care also stem from social exclusion. It is true that children of marginalised and socially excluded communities tend to populate alternative care more than those who are not. Considering the negative outcomes of most care leavers, there is a high likelihood of a cyclical nature of institutional care whereby youths who have a history of being institutionalised as children may end up having children who will be placed in state care.

Gubrium and Holstein (1993) argued that families are organisationally embedded in various agencies of social control, and how they are understood will have to take that context into consideration. This is particularly true for families who are in contact with the child welfare system. The child welfare institution, with all its systems and interactions, is the unique setting that has not been considered in most constructions of family in recent years. This neglect has also meant ignoring a large group of young people whose views on family meanings remain largely unexplored, more so in the context of Southern Africa. This leads to their continued social exclusion and marginalisation. In general, studies that have examined the family notion in nonnormative living arrangements, including out-of-home care (OOHC) settings and residential care, are few. Extant studies on the family concept in residential care have described "family" in residential care settings using phrases such as "like-family" (Kendrick, 2013), "second family" (Roche et al., 2021), and "pseudofamily centres" (Nourian et al., 2016, p.2). This may suggest the existence of relationships that may resemble family during the separation from their families of origin.

A CRITICAL SOCIAL WORK PERSPECTIVE

Considering the above, a critical social work perspective was found relevant for the study. Critical social work, from a broader perspective, is concerned with the analysis and transformation of power relations at every level of social work, including radical, Marxist, feminist and anti-oppressive practice (Healy, 2014). Modern critical social work is oriented towards the understanding of the structural conditions that impact the emergence and maintenance of social problems. I argue that the separation of children from their birth families is a sociopolitical issue. Globally, there have been calls to end child–family separation as a child rights issue. The lack of action to end the separation of children from their families poses a threat to their lives and increases their vulnerability. The institutionalisation of children has been found to be harmful to their development (Goldman et al., 2020; van IJzendoorn et al., 2020), often leading to them becoming adults who are marginalised and experience social exclusion.

Understanding the relational lives of adolescents and youths who have been separated from their birth families and living in child welfare institutions, therefore, becomes a critical social work issue. Social workers who work with institutionalised young people have to focus more on their familial relationships as an intervention that has the potential to reduce their stigmatisation in society and improve their adulthood outcomes. The way institutionalised youths relate to their birth families is influenced by the macro, structural forces that led them to being separated from their birth families in the first place, including poverty and welfare systems. A critical social work perspective provides the scope to emphasise the structural inequities that lead to separation from the birth families, the experiences in the child welfare institution and ensuing after leaving care, which have been well documented (e.g., Stein, 2012; van Breda & Frimpong-Manso, 2020).

The critical social work approach, therefore, allows us to raise questions about the particularly marginalising aspects of the child welfare system and institutional care structure, which may influence the concept of family life. A just society in which all youths, including those from disadvantaged and difficult backgrounds, have their place, then the reduction of social exclusion as an overarching goal, is worth consideration. A critical social work perspective provides a framework to reflect on current child welfare policies, practices, conformist social values and ideals that impede the social inclusion of separated youths in institutions. This also entails rethinking the existing, limiting definitions of "family" to allow for broader understandings that encompass the breadth of experiences that adolescents and youths growing up outside of family care may face.

CLARIFICATION OF KEY TERMS IN THE STUDY

"Family"

The term "family" in quotation marks describes a diverse set of dynamic relationships that shift over time. Traditionally, the commonly used phrase in family scholarship was "the family", which described a distinct unit that was made up of heterosexual parents and their two children (nuclear family). However, the emergence of diverse forms of family has led to changes in how scholars describe and articulate family as a concept to accommodate and acknowledge this diversity. Several scholars (e.g., Gubrium & Holstein, 1993; Williams, 2004; Ribbens-McCarthy et al., 2012) have used the term "family" in quotation marks to symbolise this diversity. In this book, I follow the same fashion by arguing for a broader understanding of family as it applies to adolescents and youths in child welfare institutions.

Child Welfare Institutions

Traditionally known as "orphanages" (see Foster, 1996; Mutangadura, 2000), child welfare institutions or facilities are places of safety for children and young people who are found in need of care, either due to the absence of parental or family care and/or due to circumstances such as neglect, abuse, family breakdown, among others. These institutions are often characterised by group care, where groups of children reside together and receive support in the form of accommodation, education and psychosocial support (Browne, 2009). According to Powell et al. (2004), institutional care in Zimbabwe includes juvenile correction facilities for youths in conflict with the law, probation hostels for delinquent youths and children's homes or residential child care facilities (RCCFs). In this study, the focus is on child welfare institutions, and the study did not include juvenile justice centres. The phrase "child welfare institutions" will be used interchangeably with "residential care facilities". In some cases, I also use the term "children's homes", which is synonymous.

Orphans and Vulnerable Children

The term "orphans and vulnerable children" (OVC) was introduced due to the limited usefulness of the construct of orphanhood in describing the

HIV/AIDS epidemic (Smart, 2003). UNICEF (2004) defines vulnerable children as children who have lost their parents and who:

> without the guidance and protection of their primary caregivers, are often more vulnerable and at risk of becoming victims of violence, exploitation, trafficking, discrimination or other abuses.

In this book, OVCs include abused, abandoned, neglected adolescents and youths without parental care and living in institutions. It also includes adolescents and youths living in poverty and are considered vulnerable; they have lost one or both parents and live with birth relatives or in child-headed households.

Looked-After Children

The term is used to refer to children living in alternative care in the United Kingdom (UK) (see, e.g., Holland & Crowley, 2013; Welch, 2018). This term is used only in the instances where UK literature was cited.

OUTLINE OF THE BOOK

Chapter 2 of this book will provide a background for the study of the meaning of family for Zimbabwean youths in child welfare institutions. It begins with a motivation as to why the study of family meanings is important. A brief history of the concept of family is provided to situate the study in the broader family traditions globally. It will also include the study methodology, including the study epistemology and ontology, research design, data collection methods, data analysis procedure and ethical considerations. The chapter ends with a reflexive account of the study, which is important considering the vulnerable target population of youths that was included in the study.

Chapter 3 continues with a discussion on the family concept, providing a more detailed account of the theoretical approaches around "family". The classical theoretical bases for the study were social constructionism and symbolic interactionism. These are discussed in relation to how youths may make sense of their family relationships, including the role played by concepts of sense of home, sense of belonging and family memories on family meanings. The application of these theories to understanding the construction of family meanings by youths in Zimbabwe's child welfare institutions is also included. Contemporary sociological theories of family also provided a background for the study in Zimbabwe. Afrocentric theories of Ukama and Ubuntu are also discussed in this chapter. The concepts of family practices and family display were discussed in relation to the study on family meanings by youths in Zimbabwe.

Chapter 4 examines child–family separation, which is one of the key factors influencing family meanings in the study. The chapter begins with a conceptualisation of child–family separation, followed by the impact of separation on children. This is followed by a subchapter on selected theories of child–family separation: ambiguous loss theory and attachment theory, chosen for their relevance to the topic under study. The final subsection discusses the separation of children and placement in child welfare institutions, including some of the features that distinguish institutions from family care.

Chapter 5 discusses families in southern Africa, which consists of the historical development of families in the region. It will include the changes that have taken place in South African families over the years. This provides a regional context for the study, which is followed by a localised context that discusses families in Zimbabwe. Families in Zimbabwe are discussed in the context of the protracted socioeconomic challenges that have contributed to the creation of some distinct families, such as child-headed families, grandparent-headed families and small-house families.

Chapter 6 presents and discusses the findings of the study on youths' constructions of family by definition and membership in child welfare institutions and in families. Descriptive statistics as well as multivariate statistical analysis results are presented and discussed. The qualitative results are also presented, concurrently highlighting the nuances between definitions of family by youths in institutions and youths in families. The chapter shows the diversity of family definitions that go beyond the traditional biological and legal definitions. The findings are discussed in relation to previous studies. The second subchapter in Chapter 6 discusses the findings based on youths' constructions of family membership. Similar to the analyses on family definition, both descriptive statistics and multivariate statistical analyses were conducted. Qualitative grounded analysis was also conducted, bringing out diverse constellations of family membership that include not only the biological family but also non-kin individuals. The findings on family membership are also discussed in light of previous studies.

Chapter 7 presents the conceptual framework for understanding youths' constructions of family while they are in institutional care and makes the final argument towards rethinking the meaning of family for adolescents and youths in child welfare institutions. It begins with a discussion around the challenges of conceptualising family in the context in which youths find themselves in and then follows with a description of the conceptual framework and how it can be applied. The policy and practice implications of this shift in thinking around the meaning of family are also provided. The chapter ends with the final conclusions, which, in summary, call for a broader understanding of family that goes beyond the traditional definitions of family and family membership but encompasses non-kin individuals and considers relationships based not only on consanguinity but also on affective characteristics, such as love, care and support. This "new" thinking around family is closer to the lived reality of children and young people who grow up outside of biological family care.

REFERENCES

Anglin, J. P. (2002). *Pain, normality and the struggle for congruence: Reinterpreting residential care for children and youth*. Binghamton, NY: Haworth Press.

Bengtsson, T. T., & Mølholt, A. K. (2018). Creation of belonging and non-belonging in the temporal narratives of young people transitioning out of care in Denmark. *Nordic Social Work Research, 8*(1), 54–64.

Bigombe, B., & Khadiagala, G. M. (2004). Major trends affecting families in Sub-Saharan Africa. *Alternativas. Cuadernos de Trabajo Social, 12*, 155–193.

Börjesson, U., & Torgé, C. J. (2022). "They say this is a home": the challenge of "home" in residential care settings for old and young. *Journal of Housing and the Built Environment, 37*(3), 1093–1108.

Briggs, E. C., Greeson, J. K., Layne, C. M., Fairbank, J. A., Knoverek, A. M., & Pynoos, R. S. (2012). Trauma exposure, psychosocial functioning, and treatment needs of youth in residential care: Preliminary findings from the NCTSN Core Data Set. *Journal of Child & Adolescent Trauma, 5*(1), 1–15.

Browne, K. (2009). The risk of harm to young children in institutional care. London: Save the Children. https://bettercarenetwork.org/library/particular-threats-to-childrens-care-and-protection/effects-of-institutional-care/the-risk-of-harm-to-youngpeople-in-institutional-care

Browne, K., Hamilton-Giachritsis, C., Johnson, R., & Ostergren, M. (2006). Overuse of institutional care for children in Europe. *BMJ, 332*(7539), 485–487.

Butterworth, S., Singh, S. P., Birchwood, M., Islam, Z., Munro, E. R., Vostanis, P., et al. (2017). Transitioning care-leavers with mental health needs: 'They set you up to fail!'. *Child and Adolescent Mental Health, 22*(3), 138–147.

Children International. (2022). Poverty in Africa. Retrieved August 23, 2022, from https://www.children.org/global-poverty/global-poverty-facts/africa#:~: text=Africa%3A%20a%20continent%20of%20children&text=An%20 estimated%2032.1%20million%20orphans%20live%20in%20Africa

Clark, A., Cameron, C., & Kleipoedszus, S. (2015). Sense of Place in Children's Residential Care Homes: Perceptions of Home?. *Institutionalised Children Explorations and Beyond, 2*(2), 190–209.

Csáky, C. (2009). Keeping children out of harmful institutions: Why we should be investing in family-based care. Save the Children. Retrieved November 2, 2018, from https://resourcecentre.savethechildren.net/document/keeping-children-out-harmful-institutions-why-we-should-be-investing-family-based-care/

Cutas, D., & Chan, S. (Eds.). (2012). *Families-beyond the nuclear ideal.* A&C Black Publishers Limited.

De Silva, D. H. (2007). Children needing protection: Experience from South Asia. *Archives of Disease in Childhood, 92*(10), 931–934.

Donato, L. D. J. F. C., Magalhaes, C. M. C., & da Silva Corrêa, L. (2017). Practices of Care from Educators at Institutional Shelters for Children. *Psychology, 8*(8), 1161.

Dorrer, N., McIntosh, I., Punch, S., & Emond, R. (2010). Children and food practices in residential care: Ambivalence in the 'institutional' home. *Children's Geographies, 8*(3), 247–259.

Dozier, M., Zeanah, C. H., Wallin, A. R., & Shauffer, C. (2012). Institutional care for young children: Review of literature and policy implications. *Social Issues and Policy Review, 6*(1), 1–25.

Efem, N. (2007). African Youth Charter: Prospects for the development of the African youth. In Workshop on the Appropriation, Dissemination and Implementation of Regional Instruments and Endogenous Democratic Governance and Conflict Prevention Mechanisms in West Africa, Dakar and Senegal.

Embleton, L., Ayuku, D., Kamanda, A., Atwoli, L., Ayaya, S., Vreeman, R., et al. (2014). Models of care for orphaned and separated children and upholding children's rights: Cross-sectional evidence from western Kenya. *BMC International Health and Human Rights, 14*(1), 1–18.

Espejo, A. (2015). The master key to the social inclusion of young people: Education and employment. In *Youth: Realities and challenges for achieving development with equality* (pp. 19–62). ECLAC. LC/G. 2647-P.

Foster, G. (1996). AIDS and the orphan crisis in Zimbabwe. *AIDS Analysis Africa, 6*(3), 12–13.

Frimpong-Manso, K. (2018). Building and utilising resilience: The challenges and coping mechanisms of care leavers in Ghana. *Children and Youth Services Review, 87*, 52–59.

Furey, R., & Harris-Evans, J. (2021). Work and resilience: Care leavers' experiences of navigating towards employment and independence. *Child & Family Social Work, 26*(3), 404–414.

Furstenberg, F. F. (2014). Fifty years of family change: From consensus to complexity. *The ANNALS of the American Academy of Political and Social Science, 654*(1), 12–30.

Goldman, P. S., Bakermans-Kranenburg, M. J., Bradford, B., Christopoulos, A., Ken, P. L. A., Cuthbert, C., et al. (2020). Institutionalisation and deinstitutionalisation of children 2: Policy and practice recommendations for global, national, and local actors. *The Lancet Child & Adolescent Health, 4*(8), 606–633.

Golombok, S., & Tasker, F. (2015). Socioemotional development in changing families. In *Handbook of child psychology and developmental science* (pp. 1–45). Wiley.

Gubrium, J. F., & Holstein, J. A. (1993). Family discourse, organizational embeddedness, and local enactment. *Journal of Family Issues, 14*(1), 66–81.

Gwenzi, G. D. (2019). The transition from institutional care to adulthood and independence: A social services professional and institutional caregiver perspective in Harare, Zimbabwe. *Child Care in Practice, 25*(3), 248–262.

Gwenzi, G. D. (2020). Constructing the meaning of "family" in the context of out-of-home care: An exploratory study on residential care leavers in Harare, Zimbabwe. *Emerging Adulthood, 8*(1), 54–63.

Gwenzi, G. D., & Ringson, J. (2023). "Why would they call me an orphan when I have parents": Care leavers' experiences of labelling and stereotyping whilst living in residential care facilities in Zimbabwe. *New Ideas in Psychology, 68*, 100968.

Healy, K. (2014). *Social work theories in context: Creating frameworks for practice (2nd ed.)*. Palgrave Macmillan.

Heath, S. B. (2012). *Words at work and play: Three decades in family and community life*. Cambridge University Press.

Holland, S., & Crowley, A. (2013). Looked-after children and their birth families: Using sociology to explore changing relationships, hidden histories and nomadic childhoods. *Child & Family Social Work, 18*(1), 57–66.

Kendrick, A. (2013). Relations, relationships and relatedness: Residential child care and the family metaphor. *Child & Family Social Work, 18*(1), 77–86.

Lumos. (2017). Children in institutions: The Global Picture. Retrieved April 29, 2019, from https://www.wearelumos.org/resources/children-institutions-global-picture/

MacDonald, M., Dellis, A., Mathews, S., & Marco, J. L. (2020). Implementing E-mentoring with care-experienced youth under "lock-down"—A South

African experience. *Journal of Children's Services, 15*(4), 253–258. https://doi.org/10.1108/JCS-07-2020-0032

McCall, R. B., & Groark, C. J. (2015). Research on institutionalized children: Implications for international child welfare practitioners and policymakers. *International Perspectives in Psychology: Research, Practice, Consultation, 4*(2), 142.

McNamara, P., Harvey, A., & Andrewartha, L. (2019). Passports out of poverty: Raising access to higher education for care leavers in Australia. *Children and Youth Services Review, 97*, 85–93.

Mutangadura, G. B. (2000). Household welfare impacts of mortality of adult females in Zimbabwe: Implications for policy and program development. In *A paper presented at the AIDS and Economics Symposium*. Durban: IAEN.

National Youth Policy. 2013. Retrieved January 7, 2023, from https://www.youthpolicy.org/national/Zimbabwe_2013_National_Youth_Policy.pdf

Nourian, M., Mohammadi Shahbolaghi, F., Nourozi Tabrizi, K., Rassouli, M., & Biglarrian, A. (2016). The lived experiences of resilience in Iranian adolescents living in residential care facilities: A hermeneutic phenomenological study. *International Journal of Qualitative Studies on Health and Well-being, 11*(1), 30485.

OECD. (2011). *Doing better for families*. OECD Publishing.

Pierson, J. (2010). *Tackling social exclusion* (2nd ed.). Routledge.

Powell, G., Chinake, T., Mudzinge, D., Maambira, W., Mukutiri, S., & UNICEF. (2004). Children in residential care: The Zimbabwean experience. Retrieved August 28, 2018, from https://bettercarenetwork.org/library/the-continuum-of-care/residential-care/children-in-residential-care-the-zimbabwean-experience

Quarmby, T., Sandford, R., & Pickering, K. (2019). Care-experienced youth and positive development: An exploratory study into the value and use of leisure-time activities. *Leisure Studies, 38*(1), 28–42.

Ribar, D. C. (2015). Why marriage matters for child wellbeing. *The Future of Children, 25*, 11–27.

Ribbens-McCarthy, J. R. (2012). The powerful relational language of 'family': Togetherness, belonging and personhood. *The Sociological Review, 60*(1), 68–90.

Ribbens-McCarthy, J. R., Doolittle, M., & Sclater, S. D. (2012). *Understanding family meanings: A reflective text*. Policy Press.

Roche, S., Flynn, C., & Mendes, P. (2021). 'They became my second family': Children's relational lives and relationship-based practice in residential care in the Philippines. *Child & Family Social Work, 26*(4), 652–663.

Shen, K., Cai, Y., Wang, F., & Hu, Z. (2021). Changing society, changing lives: Three decades of family change in China. *International Journal of Social Welfare, 30*(4), 453–464.

Sissay, L. (2016, December 24). Everything in life is connected, and everything is connected to family. Interview in the Guardian. Retrieved August 12, 2017, from https://www.theguardian.com/lifeandstyle/2016/dec/24/lemn-sissay-poet-christmas-dinner-childrens-homes-care-leavers

Smart, C. (2003). Towards an understanding of family change: Gender conflict and children's citizenship. *Australian Journal of Family Law, 17*(1), 1–17.

Stein, M. (2012). *Young people leaving care: Supporting pathways to adulthood.* Jessica King Publishers.

UN. (2008). General Assembly Resolutions, A/RES/62/126.

UNICEF. (2004). Children on the brink—A joint report on orphan estimates and program strategies. Retrieved October 25, 2022, from https://data.unaids.org/publications/external-documents/unicef_childrenonthebrink2004_en.pdf

Van Breda, A. D. P., & Frimpong-Manso, K. (2020). Leaving care in Africa. *Emerging Adulthood, 8*(1), 3–5.

Van IJzendoorn, M. H., Bakermans-Kranenburg, M. J., Duschinsky, R., Fox, N. A., Goldman, P. S., Gunnar, M. R., et al. (2020). Institutionalisation and deinstitutionalisation of children 1: A systematic and integrative review of evidence regarding effects on development. *The Lancet Psychiatry, 7*(8), 703–720.

Vandivere, S., Yrausquin, A., Allen, T., Malm, K., & McKlindon, A. (2012). Children in nonparental care: A review of the literature and analysis of data gaps. *Children, 12*(1).

Welch, V. (2018). Talking back to 'family', 'family troubles', and 'the looked-after child'. *Sociological Research Online, 23*(1), 197–218.

Williams, F. (2004). *Rethinking families.* Calouste Gulbenkian Foundation.

CHAPTER 2

A Study on Family Meanings

WHY STUDY FAMILY MEANINGS?

Despite the many changes that have taken place in families in the last few decades, the subject of family remains an important part of our society. Family is particularly salient for children and young people. In general terms, "family" represents many things for individual members, including being a place of safety, source of identity and social support. As Trask (2009) states, the concept of family is imbued with symbolic meaning and lived experiences, and in whatever shape or form it takes, it remains an important social group. Sociologists have also argued that family is a powerful symbol in our cultural imaginations (Holland & Crowley, 2013). For youths growing up outside of biological family care, how they construct their meanings of "family" while in separation has been neglected in the dominant family discourse.

The family, as acknowledged in the Preamble of the United Nations Convention on the Rights of the Child (UNCRC, 1989, p. 3):

is the fundamental group of society and the natural environment for the growth and well-being of all its members and particularly children, should be afforded the necessary protection and assistance so that they can fully assume their responsibilities within the community.

G. D. Gwenzi, *Rethinking the Meaning of Family for Adolescents and Youth in Zimbabwe's Child Welfare Institutions*, Palgrave Macmillan Studies in Family and Intimate Life, https://doi.org/10.1007/978-3-031-23375-3_2

and Article 20 recognises that:

A child temporarily or permanently deprived of his or her family environment, or in whose own best interests cannot be allowed to remain in that environment, shall be entitled to special protection and assistance provided by the State. (UNCRC, 1989, p.7)

Furthermore, global child welfare experts, such as UNICEF and Save the Children concur that in most cases, the best place for children to be nurtured is within a family setting. Other forms of care outside of the child's family of origin must be considered only when the family is unable or unwilling to provide care. Family has also been identified as a key context for identity formation and plays a protective role for children and young people. Family is also the foundation of young people's sociocultural and economic lives. It is a fundamental generative resource for society's material, symbolic and relational production (Donati, 2012). An individual's socioeconomic status as a child is intimately related to their family characteristics (Raphael, 2013) and predicts health outcomes during adolescence and adulthood. Furthermore, "family" is an ultimate source of survival and has traditionally been described as an *economic and social risk absorber* (Hiroko, 2008), contributing to the social and economic well-being of the individual. Family is equally important for the development of a series of relationships, including partnering, parenting, friendship and affiliation, and the connections between adult members of a family (Spicker, 2014). McDaniel, Tepperman and Colavecchia (2014, pg. 20) rightly noted that:

families provide our most important relationships, our first connection to the social world, and a connection that remains important throughout our lives.

Drawing on Finch and Mason's (2003) model of family support, there are five dimensions of care from one's family: financial and material (including cash remittances or goods such as food, clothing, and paying household and other bills), practical (exchanging advice and assisting with tasks), emotional and moral aimed at improving psychological well-being, personal care (like feeding and bathing), and accommodation (providing shelter and security). It is sufficient, then, to suggest that any significant disruption in family life can have far-reaching implications for young people and individual members of the family, which will, in turn, impact the overall well-being of whole societies. The study into the subjective meanings of "family" for adolescents and youths in child welfare institutions is therefore an area worth exploring. Childhood happiness, development, rights and entitlements in atypical families have become topics of interest for family scholars (see, e.g., Cheng & Powell, 2005; Quadlin et al., 2022; Vignoli et al., 2014), and the discourse is said to have various political and social implications (Edwards et al., 2012).

Furthermore, there are existing debates on the benefits of biological family connections and the extent to which family continuity should outweigh other economic and social advantages that may accompany non-kin placements (Barth, 1999; Bartholet, 1999).

The study also provides an opportunity to consider a model for understanding the meaning of family for young people growing up outside of biological family care, which may be useful for social work practitioners and policymakers. There is also scope to apply a critical social work perspective, highlighting the injustice of early childhood adversity, including separation from the biological family and the social exclusion that accompanies young people growing up outside of the normative family setting.

Defining Family

It is important to provide some background context relating to the social construction of family meanings, which is the focus of the study. This begins with defining what family is and proceeds to discuss why and how family definitions may vary from person to person. People define family in ways that make sense to them, their past and present realities, and their lived experiences. The way family is defined is therefore dependent on several factors, including people's contexts (geographical, sociocultural, economic, and political). This suggests that there is no standard definition of family, and in today's society, "family" means whatever the individual who is defining it wants it to mean. The language used to define family also differs across cultures; hence, assumptions cannot be made about what family means for people in those cultures. Personal understandings of whom family includes might also depend on factors such as the quality of the relationship (Becker & Charles 2006), being there at crucial life moments, or the frequency of face-to-face contact (Davies, 2012). These are all based on the premise that "family" is a facet of social life, not a social institution, and it "represents a quality rather than a thing" (Morgan, 1996: 186). These definitions signify a move away from the notion of family as being understood only on the basis of consanguinity and allow for the exploration of family relationships among non-kin individuals.

In the absence of a standard definition of family, however, there are two broad categorisations that can guide the general understanding of families over the years, namely, the traditional and nontraditional definitions.

Traditional Family Definition

The family has always been concerned with the natural and/or biological world (Ribbens-McCarthy, 2012). The traditional family was defined as a large group of kin living together, including children, parents and grandparents. The 1960s and 1970s saw a move from the traditional to what is now known as the modern family. The countercultural revolution that began in the 1960s and early 1970s both rejected and posed alternatives to nuclear family forms (Berger, 2017). According to Berger (2017, p. 12), "a coalition of special interest groups came to declare war on the conventional family and nearly succeeded in driving it into the underground". Bengtsson (2001) highlighted a number of hypotheses that were put forward in the heated debate surrounding family change in the early 1990s: a) *the nuclear family hypothesis,* which noted the shift from large to smaller family units consisting of two heterosexual parents and their child(ren) who were joined by affective ties; b) *the decline of the modern nuclear family as a social institution* due to high divorce rates during this period; and c) *the increasing heterogeneity of family forms,* incorporating relations that surpassed biological and conjugal boundaries, which introduced ideas such as kinship and families of choice (Furstenberg et al., 2020).

Arlene Skolnick in 1973 stated that the nuclear family was *alive but not well.* It was undergoing some major changes that had become noticeable. Ulrich Beck later referred to "family" as a "zombie category" that was "dead, and still alive" (Beck-Gernsheim, 2002, p. 203).

Nontraditional Family Definition

The ways people define "family" in the twentieth century have become increasingly diverse, stretching the boundaries of a previously narrower constellation (Jamieson, 2005) to become something more individually particular and subjectively constructed (Duncan et al., 2014). "Family" has become something that people "do" (Morgan 1996; 2011), rather than a fixed entity into which they were born. These changes in family definition support the heterogeneity hypothesis earlier stated, which supports various family forms. "Family" can now also include bonds between those unconnected by blood or law, such as those between friends (Roseneil, 2000; Allan & Crow, 2001; Weeks, et al., 2004; Roseneil & Budgeon, 2004), and even relationships with animals (Charles & Davies, 2011).

Sociological research has shown evidence that individual constructions of "family" now incorporate a diverse range of relationships that can be based on "blood" (i.e., biological, genetic links), on (re)marriage, which in the context of this study is the traditional definition or on coresidence and affective practices (Ribbens-McCarthy, 2012; Morgan, 2011). Due to the emerging conceptualisations of family, some sociologists have used alternative concepts to family, such as personal life (Smart, 2011), intimacy (Jamieson, 2005), relationships and families, as a plural (Lindsay & Dempsey, 2009) to accommodate the diversity of close relations now available. Some sociologists, however, argue that this move brings about further confusion about the state of the family. For instance, Edwards et al., (2012, p.2) call for the preservation of the concept of "family" as it is to preserve its true meaning for individuals.

Despite all these changes and new developments in the way society views "family", there is still a gap in the knowledge of family meanings in the context of child–family separation. Extant studies have explored family meanings in the context of transnational family separation (e.g., Baldassar et al., 2014), families living apart together (e.g., Duncan & Phillips, 2010) and family separation due to incarceration (e.g., Kuo, 2020; Miller, 2006). There, however, remains a gap in studies that explore the meaning of "family" for young people separated from their biological families and living child welfare institutions.

THE RESEARCH METHODOLOGY

This subchapter describes the methodology that was used in the study. The section will describe the research epistemology, research design, study procedure, study participants, data collection procedures, analysis, ethical considerations and some statements on the researcher's positionality.

Study Epistemology and Ontology

The meaning of "family" was viewed as a social construct in which young people's living contexts and subjective experiences played a part in how they make sense of family. This has foundations in the social construction of reality, which has roots in symbolic interactionism and social constructionism. Due to the focus on meaning-making around the concept of family, the subject of family in the study was regarded as a matter of subjective perception. As Gubrium and Holstein (1993, pg. 4) stated:

> *family is not objectively meaningful ... but rather it is constantly under construction, obtaining its defining characteristics through interactive practice.*

Social constructionism is one of the theoretical foundations for the study, and it focuses on social forces rather than individual forces shaping meanings (Young & Collin, 2004). More specifically, the study was guided by an interpretive social constructionist (ISC) philosophy and relativist ontology. Relativism is the view that "reality is subjective and differs from person to person" (Guba & Lincoln, 1994, p. 110). ISC is a more radical form of constructionism, originating from pragmatism, symbolic interactionism, phenomenology and ethnomethodology (Kham, 2013). ISC was chosen for this study because it allows for multiple perspectives drawing from a wide range of theoretical explanations (Bryman, 2012).

In the study, the construction of the meaning of "family" was not regarded as an automatic event but the outcome of social processes and interactions (Harris, 2010). In general, the constructionist approach helps to understand how family meanings are connected and experienced in any social location and how these meanings are interpreted (Gubrium & Holstein, 1993). In this view, family is produced as an interpretive practice and is, in essence, "a set of conceptual resources for accomplishing the meaning of social bonds" (Gubrium & Holstein, 1993, pg.5).

In line with the constructivist grounded theory approach, the study did not begin with a theory to prove, disprove or extend, and the concepts surrounding the meaning of family were developed through the reading and rereading of the textual data and uncovering categories within the quantitative data (Glaser, 2005). The process also involved collecting data, writing field notes and coding (Charmaz, 2006), bringing out meanings from the data. For constructivists, research findings are written up in such a way that they remain transparently grounded in the lives of those who co-constructed the data, that is, the participants and researcher (Mills et al., 2006). This allowed the researcher to be reflexive about their involvement in the study.

The study also considered adolescents and youths as the social actors, which focuses on how they construct their everyday lives and the ways they orient themselves in society, engaging with cultural performances and the social worlds they construct and take part in (Smith, 2007). The way social actors construct their social worlds and give meanings to their experiences is important. The social actor approach was used to highlight the agency of adolescents and youths in child welfare institutions in constructing their own family meanings, despite their vulnerable circumstances that are widely documented in the literature. The study participants were regarded as social actors with the ability to formulate meanings about their family lives. This was done primarily through seeking their personal views on how they defined "family" and not relying on the perspectives of their caregivers and other adults involved in their care.

Throughout the study, the complexity, nuance and subjectivity of the concept of family is highlighted. This complexity was evident from the ways in which participants described their family relationships in the context of biological family separation, as well as during the interpretation of the study findings. The complexity was also evident in the analysis of the institutional experience, considering its distinct characteristics, including being cared for by non-kin caregivers, transient relationships within the child welfare system, contact with the Children's Court system at admission and discharge from the institution, living with other young people from diverse backgrounds, and daily interactions with volunteers, donor agencies and social workers. These characteristics of the institutional environment provide a unique setting in which to investigate "family" meanings. Furthermore, as stated previously, the sociology of family provided more contemporary ways of thinking about "family" that encompassed a wide range of options of what family could be, beyond the biological family. Theoretically, the sociological concepts of *family practices* (Morgan, 2011) and *family display* (Finch, 2007) provide the framework for analysing family meanings for adolescents and youths living in child welfare institutions. Additionally, African family theory (*Ukama*) and *Ubuntu* provided a culturally relevant theoretical base for the study.

Research Design

A mixed-method research design of a convergent parallel nature was utilised. Questionnaires that contained both closed- and open-ended questions were used that combined both quantitative and qualitative components. This entailed separate analyses for the different types of data. This also involved the merging of data, looking out for convergence, divergence, contradictions or relationships.

Study Procedure

Fieldwork was carried out over a six-month period between June 2017 and January 2018. Some child welfare institutions took between three days and two weeks to return completed questionnaires, depending on the availability and numbers of participants in the selected age range. A faster response rate was recorded during school holidays and weekends when they were not in school. Participant observations were also carried out during the researcher's visits to the child welfare institutions. Initial visits were conducted to explain to groups of children what the project was about and the second visit when collecting questionnaires. A total of 22 visits were conducted. Some institutions required more than one visit to collect questionnaires, as they would report that some of them were not yet completed.

Data Collection

There were two groups of study participants: adolescents and *youths in child welfare institutions* and *in families.* The group in families was included to provide a comparative analysis with those in child welfare institutions.

Adolescents and Youths in Child Welfare Institutions

There is a lack of up-to-date data on children living in child welfare institutions in Zimbabwe. This is reportedly due to poor reporting structures and a lack of monitoring services as a result of an incapacitated social services department in the Ministry of Public Service, Labour and Social Welfare (MPLSW) (Wyatt et al., 2010). Consequently, the total population of young people living in child welfare institutions could not be determined at the time of the study. Nine child welfare institutions were included in the study, and permission to access them was provided by the

Department of Social Development, then called the Department of Social Services (DSS), in Harare. The DSS provided permission to access the child welfare institutions after conducting an ethical review. Of the nine institutions, six were state-run and three were private faith-based institutions. A total of 600 questionnaires were distributed in the nine institutions, and 465 adolescents and youths aged 13–19 completed them, giving a response rate of almost 78%.

The initial target group for the study was adolescents aged 13–17 years. The Children's Act: Chapter 5:06 of Zimbabwe states that young people are discharged from child welfare institutions at age 18. At age 18, youths are considered to be adults and are therefore not expected to remain in the child welfare institution. However, there were youths aged 18 and 19 who were found to still reside in the child welfare institutions. There are two reasons to explain this: first, youths who are still pursuing their General Certificate of Education (GCE) are often allowed to stay until they complete this level, and second, some of the child welfare institutions do not discharge children who have nowhere to go. In this case, they transfer them into transitional facilities while they learn a skill or until they access employment and are able to fend for themselves. It is imperative to note that youths aged 18 and above were found in a minority of child welfare institutions, mostly faith-based institutions. In state institutions, youths reported being discharged at 18 even if they had nowhere to go.

A 39-item self-administered questionnaire was used to collect data from adolescents and youths in child welfare institutions. The questionnaire collected data about their relationships with their birth families and other individuals in the institution using several different questions. Details about the questionnaire operationalisation are provided in the annex.

Adolescents and Youths in Families
A sample of young people living in families provided a comparison group for the group in institutions. Adolescents of the same age (13–17) who were identified as orphans and vulnerable children (OVCs) were selected for the study because they had similar circumstances to those in child welfare institutions and were at risk of being separated from family care. This sample was selected from two schools in the same location as the institutions using convenience sampling. Each school kept a list of OVCs who were on BEAM, and from this list, those who were available and willing to participate were included in the study. Personal connections were instrumental in finding school principals who were willing to have their schools

included in the study. A 26-item, self-administered questionnaire was utilised, which consisted of questions similar to the institutional questionnaire, excluding the institutional questions. From two schools, the total number of young people in the age group was 123; however, only 105 were available and willing to participate in the study. After the questionnaires were returned, only 99 questionnaires could be used, as some contained many missing data and had to be discarded.

Participants gave their assent since they were below the age of 18, and further consent had to be provided by their guardian. The researcher sent forms with the pupils with details about the study and had them signed by parents and guardians. Some adolescents in child-headed households had their forms signed by older siblings. In Chap. 4 of this book, a detailed description of child-headed families is provided to improve the reader's understanding of this phenomenon.

Family Variables for Participants in Child Welfare Institutions

Reason for Admission
Participants were asked to state the reason why they were not living in their family home. Some examples were provided to ensure understanding, such as parent(s) died, parents separated and so on. This was asked as an open-ended question, and from the responses, categories of reasons for admission were created as dummy variables.

Family Contact
Five questions in the questionnaire were related to contact with institutional participants' birth families while living in the institution. First, participants were asked whether they had had any contact with a family member during their time in the institution (Yes/No). If yes, a category question asked whom they had had contact with. A list of individuals (e.g., mother, father, aunt, uncle, grandmother, cousin) was provided for participants to tick all that applied. Participants were also asked to specify the type of contact they had with the individuals listed. Response categories were provided to assist participants in identifying types of contact based on the literature, namely, face-to-face contact in the form of visits, telephone contact and contact via social media (Facebook, WhatsApp). An open-ended option of "other" was provided in case some participants had experienced other forms of contact not included, for example,

communication in the form of letters. Last, participants were asked to describe their relationship with the individuals they had had contact with using a ranking Likert scale from excellent (5) to poor (1).

Sibling Relationships
Participants were asked whether they had a sibling (Yes/No) and, if yes, whether they were living with their sibling in the institution. Participants were also asked whether they had sibling(s) not living with them in the institution with relatives (Yes/No). The main focus was to understand whether adolescents and youths experienced sibling separation while in the institution. Sibling relationships have been reported to play a "protective role" for children living without their biological parents, helping them to maintain a sense of continuity with their original families and acting as a buffer for the stress associated with separation (Sen & Broadhurst, 2011).

Placement Instability
Institutionalised young people often experience placement instability and may have experienced living in more than one placement (Webster et al., 2000). Participants were asked if they had lived for six months or more with listed individuals (e.g., biological parents, relatives, foster parents or in another child welfare institution) from the time they were born until the time of the interview. The option "I never left the institution" was included, which also measured prior experience with the biological family and/or whether participants had lived in the child welfare institution from infancy. Additionally, this response was used to validate the length of stay in the child welfare institution.

Social Support
Participants were asked to whom they would go to for support using an open-ended question. This was left open to allow not limiting participants' options of support and allowing them to use their agency in thinking about who was a supportive individual in their lives. The literature documents positive outcomes for young people living in institutions when they have social support (e.g., Frimpong-Manso, 2017; Pinchover & Attar-Schwartz, 2018).

Data Analysis

The questionnaires contained both closed- and open-ended responses, which entailed a two-stage data analysis process. Points of integration between the qualitative and quantitative data were found based on similar or comparative data. The Statistical Package for the Social Sciences (SPSS) version 21 was used to analyse the quantitative data. Analyses included descriptive statistics, Chi-squares, binomial logistic regressions and multinomial logistic regressions. More details will be provided in subsequent sections of the book. A grounded analysis was carried out for the qualitative data using NVivo-11 Pro software. The thematic analysis involved sorting and organising the categories of data into themes emerging from the study, making interpretations and creating subthemes that followed the same patterns (Braun & Clarke, 2006).

Ethical Considerations

Young people in child welfare institutions are a marginalised and vulnerable group. They fall under the category of orphans and vulnerable children (OVCs). As such, the study had to follow standard ethical guidelines of conducting research with the vulnerable.

Gatekeepers

These individuals were key entry points for gaining access to the study participants. Unfortunately, gatekeeping agencies can prevent access to potential participants. The age groups of the participants meant that they were still minors who could not provide their own consent, which necessitated dealing with gatekeepers. Informed consent was therefore acquired through gatekeepers, in this case, participants' guardians and child welfare institution superintendents. This entailed writing formal letters seeking permission to conduct the study with this age group.

For adolescents and youths living in child welfare institutions, permission to conduct the study was sought from the Ministry of Public Service, Labour and Social Welfare (MPLSW) through the Department of Social Services (DSS). The permission letter was received after a two-month waiting period due to bureaucratic issues in the Department. The MPLSW also made the decision about which child welfare institutions could be accessed by the researcher. This increased the possibility of bias in the selection of child welfare institutions.

For participants in families who were accessed through schools, formal written application letters were also needed. Participants were also provided with consent forms to take home to their guardians to sign before commencing the study. This form included the study description and assurance of confidentiality and no harm to the young people.

Sensitive Information

The subject of family is a sensitive one, particularly for young people who have been separated from their biological families and have traumatic histories. Negative family memories can elicit emotional reactions that may possibly harm participants (Sng, 2009). This sensitivity was acknowledged, and efforts were made to ensure the protection of participants from secondary harm. The use of questionnaire methodology ensured no direct contact with participants as they were completing the questionnaires. Careful attention was given to the language used in the questionnaire so as not to be intrusive. The questions used in the questionnaire did not ask participants to provide any extensive details about their life experiences beyond defining what and who is "family" for them. There was a possibility that the young participants would detail experiences of current or past abuse in the child welfare institution. In this case, the consent form included a statement stating that the researcher had a moral obligation to report any disclosures of abuse or threats of harm.

Gatekeepers also ensured the protection of adolescent participants in child welfare institutions by only allowing the use of questionnaires and forbidding direct interviews with minors. Face-to-face methods of data collection can impede the sharing of sensitive information. Participants may have felt uncomfortable sharing their family experiences with a complete stranger, which would have necessitated multiple sessions of rapport-building before the commencement of data collection. The questionnaire methodology left room for participants to be completely open in completing the questionnaires. Participants did this at their convenience in their institutions, with caregivers they were comfortable with. This was done to reduce the risk of young people experiencing secondary harm through direct contact with the researcher.

Participants were also informed of their voluntary participation and that they would not be forced to complete the questionnaires. The caregivers reported that some of the young people did decline to fill in the questionnaires, hence the response rate of 78% of the total number sent to the institutions.

The consent form also included an assurance of confidentiality and anonymity, which meant that no real names of participants or child welfare institutions would be published. Instead, each participant was provided with a pseudonym, and these will be used throughout this book. After data collection and entry, raw data were kept on a password-protected computer and labelled with identifying codes only known to myself. Anonymised data files were only shared with the Doctoral Supervision Committee and data entry assistant.

Younger Children

Doing research with young children always requires careful ethical considerations. When designing the study, the researcher decided to focus on adolescents aged 13–17 and older youths instead of younger children aged 12 and below. This age group was specifically chosen due to their increased ability to fill in the questionnaires under supervision compared to younger children who may have cognitive and language limitations (Scott, 2008). The study did not involve young people with known mental and physical disabilities whose cognitive abilities may have been compromised or who would have found it difficult to participate in the study. Questionnaires can generally be used with children aged 12–16 (Scott, 2008). The researcher still had to ensure that there was little to no ambiguity in the wording of the questions.

RESEARCHER REFLEXIVITY

Reflexivity is defined as a conscious process of self-reflection in which the researcher acknowledges their position and the role they may have played in influencing the study findings (Darkwah, 2018; Davies, 2008). Reflexivity refers to the researcher being aware of any social, political, linguistic or ideological origins of their own perspective and voice as well as the voices of the participants and those to whom the research will be disseminated (Patton, 2002).

Coming from a social work background, with specific experience of working with orphans and vulnerable young people in child welfare institutions meant that I was well positioned to understand, at a foundational level, the lives of the researched. I was also comfortable entering the research environment, as it was one I had become familiar with from both a practice and research point of view. Having previously conducted research in child welfare institutions (Masters' thesis, 2015), some relationships with institutions in Zimbabwe were formed. However, the challenges arose from my position as an "outsider" (I was conducting research in Zimbabwe after having lived outside of the country as an international student for over a decade). This was despite the fact that I am a native who speaks the same language as the study participants. However, efforts were made to become acquainted with the research environment and the young people involved prior to commencing the study.

CONCLUSION

To understand the study on which this book is based, this chapter provides a background for the study of family meanings, beginning with the rationale for the study. How family is being defined in the study was also detailed since there are many different ways to study family. It was clarified that family meanings in this study refer to two constructs: family definition and family membership. The traditional definition of family was provided, followed by the nontraditional definition. These definitions provided the background to understand what is meant by family in this book, including the philosophical underpinnings of the study. The chapter also discussed the study methodology, including the research design, data collection tools and procedures, data analysis and ethical considerations. The chapter ended with a reflexive account that detailed the researcher's positionality during the study, which contributes to ensuring that the research was conducted ethically and with rigour.

REFERENCES

Allan, G., & Crow, G. (2001). *Families, households and society*. Palgrave.

Baldassar, L., Kilkey, M., Merla, L., & Wilding, R. (2014). Transnational families. *The Wiley Blackwell companion to the sociology of families*, 155–175.

Barth, R. (1999). After safety, what is the goal of child welfare services: Permanency, family continuity or social benefit? *International Journal of Social Welfare*, 8(4), 244–252.

Bartholet, E. (1999). *Nobody's children: Abuse and neglect, foster drift, and the adoption alternative*. Beacon.

Beck-Gernsheim, E. (2002). *Reinventing the family: In search of new lifestyles*. Polity.

Becker, B., & Charles, N. (2006). Layered meanings: The construction of 'the family' in the interview. *Community, Work and Family, 9*(2), 101–122.

Berger, B. (2017). *The family in the modern age: More than a lifestyle choice.* Routledge.

Bengtsson, V. L. (2001). Beyond the nuclear family: The increasing importance of multigenerational bonds: The burgess award lecture. *Journal of Marriage and Family, 63*(1), 1–16.

Braun, V., & Clarke, V. (2006). Using thematic analysis in psychology. *Qualitative Research in Psychology, 3*(2), 77–101.

Bryman, A. (2012). *Social research methods* (4th ed.). Oxford University Press.

Charles, N., & Davies, C. A. (2011). My family and other animals: pets as kin. In *Human and other animals* (pp. 69–92). Palgrave Macmillan, London.

Charmaz, K. (2006). *Constructing grounded theory: A practical guide through qualitative analysis.* Sage.

Cheng, S., & Powell, B. (2005). Small samples, big challenges: Studying atypical family forms. *Journal of Marriage and Family, 67*(4), 926–935.

Darkwah, E. (2018). *"Caring for parentless" children: An exploration of work-related experiences of caregivers in children's homes in Ghana.* Doctoral Dissertation. University of Bergen, Norway.

Davies, H. (2008). Reflexivity in research practice: Informed consent with children at school and at home. *Sociological Research Online, 13*(4), 1–14. https://doi.org/10.5153/sro.1775

Davies, H. (2012). Affinities, seeing and feeling like family: Exploring why children value face-to-face contact. *Childhood, 19*(1), 8–23.

Donati, P. (2012). *Relational Sociology: A New Paradigm for the Social Sciences.* Routledge.

Duncan, S., & Phillips, M. (2010). People who live apart together (LATs)–how different are they?. *The sociological review, 58*(1), 112–134.

Duncan, S., Phillips, M., Carter, J., Roseneil, S., & Stoilova, M. (2014). Practices and perceptions of living apart together. *Family Science, 5*(1), 1–10. https://doi.org/10.1080/19424620.2014.927382

Edwards, R., McCarthy, J. R., & Gillies, V. (2012). The politics of concepts: family and its (putative) replacements. *The British Journal of Sociology, 63*(4), 730–746.

Finch, J. (2007). Displaying families. *Sociology, 41*(1), 65–81.

Finch, J. V., & Mason, J. (2003). *Negotiating family responsibilities.* Routledge.

Frimpong-Manso, K. (2017). The social support networks of care leavers from a children's village in G hana: formal and informal supports. *Child & Family Social Work, 22*(1), 195–202.

Furstenberg, F. F., Harris, L. E., Pesando, L. M., & Reed, M. N. (2020). Kinship practices among alternative family forms in Western industrialized societies. *Journal of Marriage and Family, 82*(5), 1403–1430.

Glaser, B. G. (2005). *The grounded theory perspective III: Theoretical coding*. Sociology Press.

Guba, E. G., & Lincoln, Y. S. (1994). Competing paradigms in qualitative research. In *Handbook of qualitative research*, 2 (163–194), 105. Sage.

Gubrium, J. F., & Holstein, J. A. (1993). Family discourse, organizational embeddedness, and local enactment. *Journal of Family Issues, 14*(1), 66–81.

Harris, S. R. (2010). *What is constructionism? Navigating its use in sociology*. Retrieved August 23, 2022, from https://www.rienner.com/title/What_Is_Constructionism_Navigating_Its_Use_in_Sociology%20?iframe=true&width=100%&height=100%

Hiroko, T. (2008). Structural reform of the family and the neo-liberalisation of everyday life in Japan. *New Political Economy, 13*(2), 153–172.

Holland, S., & Crowley, A. (2013). Looked-after children and their birth families: Using sociology to explore changing relationships, hidden histories and nomadic childhoods. *Child & Family Social Work, 18*(1), 57–66.

Jamieson, L. (2005). Boundaries of intimacy. In *Families in society boundaries and relationships* (pp. 188–206). https://doi.org/10.1332/policypress/9781861346438.003.0011

Kham, T. V. (2013). Overview of social constructionism and its potential applications for social work education and research in Vietnam. *Journal of Social Sciences and Humanities, 29*(4), 30–37.

Kuo, K. (2020). Family separation and incarceration: An intersectional analysis of the carceral system. Doctoral dissertation, The University of Wisconsin-Milwaukee.

Lindsay, J., & Dempsey, D. (2009). *Families, and intimate life*. Oxford University Press.

McDaniel, S. A., & Tepperman, L. (2014). *Close relations: An introduction to the sociology of families*. Pearson Education Canada.

Miller, K. M. (2006). The impact of parental incarceration on children: An emerging need for effective interventions. *Child and Adolescent Social Work Journal, 23*(4), 472–486.

Mills, J., Bonner, A., & Francis, K. (2006). The development of constructivist grounded theory. *International Journal of Qualitative Methods, 5*(1), 25–35.

Morgan, D. H. (1996). *Family connections: An introduction to family studies*. Polity.

Morgan, D. (2011). *Rethinking family practices*. Springer.

Patton, M. (2002). *Qualitative research and evaluation methods (3rd ed.)*. Thousand Oaks, CA: Sage Publications.

Pinchover, S., & Attar-Schwartz, S. (2018). Is someone there for you? Social support of youth in educational residential care from family, peers and staff. *The British Journal of Social Work, 48*(8), 2195–2214. https://doi.org/10.1093/bjsw/bcx164

Quadlin, N., Jeon, N., Doan, L., & Powell, B. (2022). Untangling perceptions of atypical parents. *Journal of Marriage and Family*.

Raphael, D. (2013). Adolescence as a gateway to adult health outcomes. *Maturitas, 75*(2), 137–141.

Ribbens-McCarthy, J. R. (2012). The powerful relational language of 'family': Togetherness, belonging and personhood. *The Sociological Review, 60*(1), 68–90.

Roseneil, S. (2000). Queer frameworks and queer tendencies: towards an understanding of postmodern transformations of sexuality. *Sociological Research Online, 5*(3), 58–70.

Roseneil, S., & Budgeon, S. (2004). Cultures of intimacy and care beyond 'the family': Personal life and social change in the early 21st century. *Current sociology, 52*(2), 135–159.

Scott, J. (2008). Children as respondents: The challenge for quantitative methods. In *Research with children* (pp. 103–124). Routledge.

Sen, R., & Broadhurst, K. (2011). Contact between children in out-of-home placements and their family and friends networks: A research review. *Child & Family Social Work, 16*(3), 298–309.

Smart, C. (2011). *Close relationships and personal life*. Palgrave MacMillan. Basingstoke.

Smith, A. (2007). Children as social actors: An introduction. *The International Journal of Children's Rights, 15*(1), 1–4.

Sng, R. (2009). Family therapy for kids without families: Working systemically with children and young people in residential care. *Australian and New Zealand Journal of Family Therapy, 30*(4), 247–259.

Spicker, P. (2014). *Social policy: Theory and practice, 167*, p. 12). Bristol: Policy Press.

Trask, B. (2009). *Globalization and families: Accelerated systemic social change*. New York, NY: Springer Science & Business Media.

UNCRC. (1989). United Nations Convention on the Rights of the Child. Retrieved May 25, 2022, from https://www.unicef.org.uk/wp-content/uploads/2010/05/UNCRC_united_nations_convention_on_the_rights_of_the_child.pdf

Webster, D., Barth, R. P., & Needell, B. (2000). Placement stability for children in out-of-home care: A longitudinal analysis. *Child Welfare, 79*, 614–632.

Vignoli, D., Pirani, E., & Salvini, S. (2014). Family constellations and life satisfaction in Europe. *Social indicators research, 117*(3), 967–986.

Weeks, J., Heaphy, B., & Donovan, C. (2004). *The lesbian and gay family. The Blackwell companion to the sociology of families*, 340–355.

Wyatt, A., Mupedziswa, R., & Rayment, C. (2010). Institutional capacity assessment: Department Of child welfare and probation services. Harare. Final Report. Ministry of Labour and Social Services.

Young, R., & Collin, A. (2004). Introduction: Constructivism and social constructionism in the career field. *Journal of Vocational Behaviour, 64*(3), 373–388.

CHAPTER 3

Theorising Family Meanings

This chapter examines the family meaning-making process. This includes a consideration of the core assumptions and thinking around the notion of "family" as well as any new meanings that may emerge in the event of a disturbance of the norm. It also includes a discussion around the key theories and concepts of family and how these may be applied to the construction of family meanings by adolescents and youths in Zimbabwe. Theories bring together things in a way that helps us understand the social world (Abend, 2008).

Meaning-making has been described as a social process, challenging the notion that it is an individual process (Davis et al., 2012). This implies that individuals create meanings based on a collaborative process, and some meanings are inherited from the social environment. However, this does not nullify subjective meanings created by individuals, but the shared meanings contribute to the individual ones. In the Zimbabwe study with adolescents and youths living in child welfare institutions and in families, meaning-making was considered a group process, and family meanings that were provided were taken to be common to the group. As described earlier, the participants involved in the study are regarded as a vulnerable group based on their adverse childhood experiences and time spent outside of biological family care. Family meanings were therefore

© The Author(s), under exclusive license to Springer Nature Switzerland AG 2023
G. D. Gwenzi, *Rethinking the Meaning of Family for Adolescents and Youth in Zimbabwe's Child Welfare Institutions*, Palgrave Macmillan Studies in Family and Intimate Life, https://doi.org/10.1007/978-3-031-23375-3_3

co-constructed through interaction and experiences with the individuals around them, including other young people in the institution. This shared understanding contributes significantly to the meanings that young people attach to certain experiences.

The psychological meanings of family can be affected when something happens in the family. For instance, in the case of family disruption, an individual may question where they now belong and who will remain in their family in that context. Boss (2006) describes the *psychological family*, which refers to an individual's basic beliefs about which people are members within one's family.

Family meanings can also change over time, which implies that the meaning-making process is fluid. The meanings an individual ascribes to their family at one stage of their life may not be the same in another stage. Family dynamics shift and change as relationships and needs evolve (McDaniel et al., 2019). The life course approach helps us to understand family changes over time (see, e.g., Hofferth and Goldscheider, 2016; Thomson et al., 2013). This creates a space for one's personal definition of family to evolve, especially for institutionalised young people who are exposed to multiple caregivers and peers who assume familial roles. Previous studies have noted the importance of family for young people, highlighting how family relationships are a primary source of meaning in life that contribute to their sense of meaning (Lambert et al., 2010).

Classical Sociological Theories of Family

There are several classical theories of family propounded by sociologists. These include functionalism, conflict theories and feminist theories. Social constructionism and symbolic interactionism were found to be relevant to the present study on family meanings.

Social Constructionism

One of the basic theories of family, social constructionism, originated from Berger and Luckmann's (1967) *Social Construction of Reality* and the *Social Construction of What?* (Hacking & Hacking, 1999). These are the foundations behind understanding how a thing becomes what it is. What do we mean when we say things are socially constructed? Ian Hacking differentiated between the social construction of ideas and objects. In this case, family is viewed as a notion or idea that is the claim as a product of a sociohistorical process. The notion can be passed down through education and from the social context. With their work on social institutions, Miranda and Saunders (2003) proposed that social institutions are an objective reality and are social constructions. Schutz (1972) stated earlier that the setting in which information is encountered contributes to its meaning; hence, there is no objectivity. For an interpretive scholar, the meaning ascribed to an idea depends on the perspectives and purposes that people bring to it. For example, when researching family meanings, one has to consider the different perspectives of participants and the purpose that family serves for them. This is interpretive social constructionism (ISC). Social constructionism, therefore, holds to the belief that there are different meanings for different individuals based on their social setting. For instance, with institutionalised children, their living arrangement and social context come with a label attached to them as being "orphans" or social misfits (Calheiros, Garrido, Lopes & Patricio et al., 2015), which is a social construct.

The social construction of family was first introduced by Gubrium and Holstein (1993), who noted that the meanings individuals ascribe to family are influenced by their social environments and thus do not occur in isolation. In addition, from the social constructionist perspective, individuals participate actively in their society and in social construction. Hence, they actively participate in the meaning-making process. Studies on the social construction of "family" have focused on how family is defined, how family life is maintained and how family practices are enacted by different groups of people. Over the last two decades, sociologists and family researchers have questioned the traditional ontological and epistemological assumptions of family research by approaching it from a social constructionist perspective. Additionally, the life experiences of young people in modern societies have changed significantly, and these changes have also influenced their views on family relations, friends, education and labour experiences, leisure and lifestyles and the ability to become established as independent young adults (Furlong & Cartmel, 2006). For young people, the effects of these social changes brought about by globalisation, industrialisation and urbanisation are usually played out in the context of family life (Lappegård et al., 2014). These changes have important implications for the conceptualisation of family by children and young people.

Some examples include literature that focuses on separated children, including children of incarcerated parents (Turney, 2017; Wildeman et al.,

2016). Some studies have focused on "family practices" in the context of family changes, such as when child–parent separation occurs (e.g., Jardine, 2017, 2018) and separation due to migration, focusing on asylum-seeking and refugee families (Rousseau et al., 2004). Recent migration studies have also focused on "doing family" from a distance (e.g., Merla et al., 2021; Yi, 2019; Studies of transnational families; although they provide crucial information on how "family" is practised in the context of separation, they do not focus on children's experiences of that separation). There remains a gap in the social construction of family meanings and practices after child–family separation and placement into a child welfare institution.

Symbolic Interactionism

Symbolic interactionism is the second relevant classical theory of family in sociology, which provides a way to examine the interactions taking place between children in institutions and the individuals in their lives. In mutual interactions, family members arrive at an understanding of one another (Hess et al., 2017). Young people in child welfare institutions may be exposed to multiple relationships with different individuals during their childhood, which may mean that they are engaged in multiple interactions. However, studies have shown evidence of limited quality interactions between institutionalised children and caregivers (e.g., Bettmann et al., 2015; McCall, 2013; McCall & Groark, 2015). Symbolic interactionism helped to explain participants' interactions within the multiple relationships they may have been exposed to. Due to its focus on meanings and definitions, symbolic interactionism provided a theoretical lens with which to understand who could be considered "family" among the group of individuals in the lives of the study participants and what would have contributed to them being assigned that membership.

Previous studies have applied a symbolic interactionist perspective to explore what symbols can make an individual to be considered part of a "family". Davies (2011), for instance, describes *naming practice* as a factor in how children identify themselves with their family members, for instance, through surnames. This naming is a "family practice" that structures children's lives and experiences. Zanette and Manrubia (2001) investigated family names as the *vertical transmission* of culture. One's family identity can also be derived from their family name (Suter et al., 2008). There remains a gap in the literature on how family names can contribute to the identity of institutionalised young people.

Winter and Cohen (2005) note how a previously looked-after young person can develop identity issues because they lack knowledge about their family origins. Some institutionalised children and young people may have been abandoned at birth and may not have knowledge of their original family names. Similarly, places have been found to hold symbolic meanings that have implications for the well-being of individuals (Jack, 2015). From a young age, children develop feelings about their surroundings, with specific attachments forming towards people and places that are consistently associated with a sense of security and other positive experiences. A child's secure base is therefore connected to their attachment base and their sense of belonging and identity.

Sense of Belonging

The need to belong is a strong interpersonal motive that influences human behaviour, emotions and thoughts (Wilczyńska et al., 2015). Belongingness is defined as "personal involvement in a social system so that persons feel themselves to be an indispensable and integral part of the system" (Anant, 1966, p. 21). Human beings have an inherent need to belong to a group that provides them with an identity, which also makes us feel connected. For children, a sense of belonging, not only to the family but also to the community, nation and larger environment, is critical. For adolescents, a sense of belonging is essential for their positive adjustment.

The sense of belonging therefore has a bearing on the construction of family meanings. Families have, for centuries, been providing individuals with a sense of belonging and identity. Hence, when families break down, this sense of belonging is also compromised. This is especially the case for young people in out-of-home care, including foster care and residential/institutional care. Hedin (2014) investigated the sense of belonging for young people in kinship families, non-relative care (but previously known by the young people) and those in traditional foster care. The study found that young people felt a sense of belonging to both the foster family and birth family. This was attributed to family practices within the foster family, such as routine dinners and sharing fun and laughter together (Hedin, 2014).

The sense of belonging is also impacted by several factors, including the social exclusion that young people experience. A study by Farmer et al. (2013) investigated children's and young people's views of being brought up in informal kinship care. They found that children and young people experienced bullying and stigmatisation due to living without parents. This had an effect on their sense of belonging in the out-of-home placement.

The review found some studies on the sense of belonging of young people separated from their birth families in the sub-Saharan African context. A study by Addae (2020) provided empirical evidence on the role of familial social capital as a potential health asset for the life satisfaction and happiness of adolescents in Ghana. The study found that social capital within the home context is a more significant protective health asset for the life satisfaction and happiness of Ghanaian adolescents. A follow-up study (Addae, 2020) investigated the impact of socioeconomic background on young people's family sense of belonging. The study found that adolescents from high socioeconomic backgrounds were protected against a low family sense of belonging compared to those from a low socioeconomic background (Addae, 2020). This implies that poverty has an impact on young people's family sense of belonging. This family sense of belonging also changes with increasing age, with older youths having a lower sense of belonging than younger children. Family sense of belonging has also been studied among transnational families (e.g., Chereni, 2015; McGregor, 2008; Mlotshwa, 2019). However, there is a dearth of studies on the relationship between sense of belonging and the construction of family meanings for institutionalised young people.

Sense of Home

An individual's sense of home affects their overall well-being, as it is related to their interaction with the environment and space. The place of residence, moving and change of residence are closely related to children's daily lives (Andenæs, 2012). A sense of home carries multiple meanings. Home depicts an intersection of place, time and social relationships that are closely connected to an emotional sense of belonging (Kauko & Forsberg, 2018). Home also provides an individual with a sense of security, permanence and continuity, reflects one's identity, provides a refuge from the outside world and represents the individual's relationships with family and friends (Després, 1991). These characteristics of home are central to understanding why young people in child welfare institutions may find it difficult to feel a sense of home in the institution. In particular, there is a notion that home is not limited to a physical place; it can be a memory or a state of mind; hence, it is a sense of home, much like a sense of belonging (ibid). A place of residence also does not become a home if it does not feel like a home. This is relevant for young people living in institutions who may find it difficult to build a sense of home and belonging in the institution. Similar notions may be found among homeless and displaced youths.

The search for literature on the sense of home for young people in out-of-home care only resulted in a few studies that focused on residential/institutional care. Most of the available studies focused on foster care. This lack of attention to the meaning of home and family for institutionalised young people further highlights their marginalisation in our society. Biehal (2014) investigated the meaning of family and home for young people in foster care. The study found that the lives of young people living in out-of-home care are characterised by much uncertainty and change, which in turn affects their sense of belonging and sense of home because it is often disrupted. Some of the young people would experience what she termed "provisional belonging" because their placements are uncertain (Biehal, 2014, p. 963). The lack of permanency in most residential care placements impacts young people's sense of home. Samuels (2009) investigated the ambiguous loss of home for young people in foster care. The study found that young people who experience chronic ambiguous loss of were impacted in how they viewed their family relationships affected their sense of agency regarding familial relationships, and this went on even into adulthood.

Family Memories

These belong primarily to the field of communicative memory, which focuses on everyday life, face-to-face interaction and oral communication, and spans approximately three to four generations (Erll, 2011). Memories are used in the construction of families within a sociocultural context (Erkonan, 2016). Symbolic interactionism states that individuals can derive meaning from their memories and can either retain that knowledge or form new negotiated meanings (Panicker, et al., 2020). Young people in out-of-home care may have both negative and positive memories of the time spent with their biological families due to their traumatic histories (McCormack & Issaakidis, 2018). However, most young people in care are reluctant to revisit painful memories of abuse or maltreatment (Fox & Berrick, 2007). Memories (good or bad) can be used to form family meanings, depending on how they are perceived by the individual.

CONTEMPORARY SOCIOLOGICAL THEORIES OF FAMILY

The sociology of family contributed immensely to the study's conceptual framework. In particular, the contemporary concepts of *family display* and *family practice* offered a viable explanation for the social construction of "family" by adolescents and youths who have been separated from their birth families and living in child welfare institutions. The separation from the birth family and ensuing placement in a child welfare institution places adolescents and youths in a nontraditional care setting that does not strictly fit into the traditional care model of the nuclear family. Historically, the dominant approaches around the family in sociology included symbolic interactionism, the family development framework, the systems framework, conflict theories and structural functionalism. These theories also focused on a single unit, usually heterosexual, that had the same functions of care, safety, socialisation and maintenance of social order. Contemporary family studies, however, have made room for great diversity and nuanced ways of thinking about families and personal relationships. In the Zimbabwe study, the sociology of family allowed the researcher to uncover the possibilities of different constellations of relationships that can be described as "family" by adolescents and youths separated from their birth families.

As seen in the discussion on ambiguous loss, the birth family remains present in the minds and hearts of young people even though they may be physically absent due to the requirements of the separation. How then do adolescents and youths construct family meanings in this context, also considering the multiple relationships they are engaged in while they are part of the child welfare system? Another key aspect that the sociology of family offers to this study is the idea that family relationships are fluid so that the people who are considered as constituting "family" also change over time. This was important considering not only the transient relationships that young people in care have with the different individuals who come into their lives but also their changing identities as they go through the life course. Additionally, the challenges that are usually present in the birth family could also improve at different stages within the life of the young person; hence, their idea of "family" need not be fixed but can also change depending on the circumstances. This is contrary to the idea of the traditional nuclear family that was idealised to the point that the idea of it being dysfunctional and possibly abusive to the care and well-being of its members was once unheard of.

In summary, the ways in which people define family in the twentieth century have become increasingly diverse, stretching the boundaries of a previously narrower constellation (Jamieson, 2005) to become something more individually particular and subjectively constructed (Duncan et al., 2014). Unfortunately, this diversity and change in "family" have not been well studied in the context of Southern Africa. Even fewer studies have examined the relevance of these contemporary family concepts to the African context (e.g., Kassa, 2016). In fact, the study by Kassa (2016) was one of the few in the African context that addressed not only the conceptualisation of family but also the missing voice of African children in family literature.

Family Practices

The *family practices* concept was useful in understanding how families can be understood by young people living in child welfare institutions. Morgan (2011) proposed that "family" can be understood through everyday practices and that the relations within families can also change between time and space. This idea, also known as "doing family", essentially means that family can be considered a *practice* and not a *thing*. Contemporary family sociologists have examined this concept and further developed it, which further signifies a shift in the way we think about families. For instance, Finch (2007, pg. 66) notes how *family practices* emphasise "social actors creatively constituting their own social world" and that the understanding of family could change over time depending on the individual's circumstances and experiences. This leaves room for negotiating and renegotiating family meanings after something disrupts the family, for example, divorce or separation (Smart & Neale, 1999). Finch and Mason (1993) investigated how relationships are negotiated based on their quality and how they are expressed in practical terms, which is, in other words, *family practices*.

Families are not normatively defined; rather, they are constructed on the basis of interactions and negotiated over time (Gillies, 2003). Jones and Hackett (2011) highlight how complex the meanings of family practices can be and their role in the construction of adoptive kinship. This provides a background for understanding the complexity in constructing the meaning of family in the context of biological family separation. As Kendrick (2013) notes, understanding the complexity of *family practices* is important for social workers working with young people in residential care.

Examples of *family practices* include the provision of support and meaningful contact between individuals, which can be key identifiers of whether one can be considered "family". This goes beyond the blood relationship to include individuals who are unrelated. *Family practices* may also include different kinds of actions that are perceived to be akin to what a family member must do, such as visiting each other, sharing things and being together. The *family practices* approach is more focused on day-to-day interactions as opposed to formal prescriptions of what a family should be or look like. Scholars who have applied the concept of *family practices* in their research (see, e.g., Hockey & James, 2017; Kendrick, 2013; Punch & McKintosh, 2014; Jones & Hackett, 2011) have not sought to presume a definition of what family is but mostly to discover what family means to the social actors involved in constructing "family" meanings.

FAMILY DISPLAY

This is another useful concept for understanding how individuals make sense of their family relationships. Finch (2007) begins with a recognition of Morgan's concept of *doing family* or *family practices*. As with *family practices, family display* analyses contemporary families based on their fluidity, diversity and multifaceted nature (p. 66). Finch expanded on family practices by adding that families need to be *displayed* as well as *done*. Meaning is created through communication and interaction with others. While displaying "family", the focus is on relationship quality, which shows that family definitions are highly dependent upon an individual's own understanding of "family" (Fowler, 2016). Macdonald (2016) applied *family display* in a study with adoptive families who were experiencing changes and additions to their family groups. Macdonald (2016, p.10), like other scholars (see, e.g., Jones & Logan, 2013; Mason, 2011), acknowledged that kinship is "made, not given", especially when considered in the context of adoption. By applying the *family display* concept, Macdonald (2016) was able to show how adoptive parents configured their families in response to the structural, social and emotional constraints they encountered after adopting. Fowler (2016) applied the *family display* concept in her study on residential care workers. She examined how they made sense of their relationships with young people in care and found that they likened it to "family".

It is important to note that young people in child welfare institutions may be engaged in *family display* without even knowing it, and these interactions and relationships can be described as "family". Other practices, such as being close together, can also make individuals feel they are a family even if they are not related by blood or marriage. This signifies another move away from the heteronormative definition of family, which placed emphasis on blood relations and the nuclear family unit with a heterosexual couple and their children. This display of family allows individuals to gain approval and recognition of their family as being just as relevant as any other (Finch, 2007). In the Zimbabwe study, *family display* may be useful due to the nature of the child welfare system and the relationships of youths with their birth families. Contact and interaction were key aspects during the young people's stay in the institution.

Linking the two concepts of family practices and family display with the work on children's conceptualisation of family and "family-like" relationships as previously done by Kendrick (2013) can assist in the development of a framework for residential staff to think about their roles and relationships with children and young people. The question of interest in this book is whether these contemporary ideas of "family" can be applied to the relational lives of young people in institutional care and, if so, how. As will be discussed in the final part of this book, a model to understand the meaning of "family" for separated adolescents and youths living in child welfare institutions may be useful.

African Family Theory (Ukama)

In the Shona culture, the concept of *ukama*, which originates from Zimbabwe (Le Grange, 2012), forms the basis of African family theory. Under this theory, family is understood within the context of relatedness or *ukama* in Shona. Ukama also consists of closeness and affection, and the individuals whom one is related to by blood or marriage are referred to as *hama or* relatives in English, which is similar to the Western ideas of "family" described in the sections above. However, in the Shona culture, *ukama* is not restricted to blood relatives (Murove, 2009) but extends to ties with all people from generations past and present (Le Grange, 2012).

Hungwe and Tofirepi (2021) further add to the definition of *ukama*, social interconnectedness and bonding within the framework of family, extended family, totem-sharing and intermarriage structure. The social interconnectedness that transcends consanguine and biolegal relations partly supports contemporary Western family definitions of relatedness (Carsten, 2004; Sørensen & Guarnizo, 2007), close relationships

(Hazan & Shaver, 1994; Smart & Neale, 1999) and personal communities (Pahl & Spencer, 2004, 2010). Murove (2007) suggests that *ukama* provides the foundation on which to understand an individual's social, spiritual and ecological togetherness. The theory provides a way to understand the social construction of family meanings by adolescents and youths in child welfare institutions in Zimbabwe, more so because it originated from the same cultural context of the adolescents and youths in the study. *Ukama*, although founded within the Shona culture, is also applicable to most African communal, relational value systems (Ndofirepi & Shanyanana, 2016), including the widely accepted *Ubuntu* notion. It describes the way relations are constructed and played out every day through social practices.

Ubuntu and African Family Values

The family was, historically, the centre of the socialisation, culture and welfare of all its members (Clausen, 1966). It held a lot of meaning for its members, and to a large extent, it still does. In the African context, Ubuntu and being connected to one's family and community are core values that continue to signify one's identity (Hailey, 2008; Siqwana-Ndulo, 1998). The family was where cultural values were taught and practised. A child who had no morals was often described as "*anobva kumba kusina vanhu*", which is loosely translated as "he/she comes from where there are no people". This was to say that their actions did not show evidence of discipline or guidance. Such symbolism was and is still crucial in the Zimbabwean African context, and evidence is seen through scholars who have evaluated the impact of institutionalisation on children based on the lack of cultural values and indiscipline because they are, in most cases, raised outside of the African culture (e.g., Dziro et al., 2013; Gwenzi, 2019; Muzingili & Gunha, 2017). Child welfare institutions are therefore viewed as a Western model of welfare that goes against our traditional values and ways of welfare.

The family was also the place in which the welfare and protection of children were enacted and practised. Local customs dictated that the nuclear and extended family had a responsibility for the welfare of its members, including OVCs (Mildred, 2014). In general, in the African context, the concept of an orphan did not exist, as the responsibility of all community members was to care for each other under the concept of Ubuntu. The adage "it takes a village to raise a child" has its origins in this communal approach to child welfare, which ensured that no child went without adequate care, even after the loss of their primary caregiver. As stated by Mafumbate (2019, p. 7):

> *In the African traditional family, the community is the custodian of the individual; hence the individual has to go where the community goes. There was a sense of belonging that came from being part of the larger community, and all social problems that would arise were therefore the community's responsibility.*

This is supported by Waghid et al. (2005, pg. 108), who state that the slogan "your child is mine [and] my child is yours" is African, and in many ways, it epitomises the sense of community that is prevalent in African society. The emergence of orphanages, which were the first form of child welfare institutions, was therefore viewed as un-African and going against the principles of Ubuntu. One of the ways in which orphanages went against Ubuntu principles was by separating OVCs from their communities and culture and raising them in the Western way of life (Dziro & Rufurwokuda, 2013). Increasingly, Zimbabwean scholars have called for a return to principles such as communalism, oneness and brotherhood within social work and, in particular, child welfare as a way of decolonising the welfare of children (e.g., Kurevakwesu & Maushe, 2020; Mugumbate & Chereni, 2020).

CONCLUSION

This chapter discussed the meaning-making process around the subject of "family". It defined how meanings of family can be constructed and factors that may influence the process. Meaning-making is described as a social process that becomes key, especially after a traumatic event, as individuals attempt to make sense of their present circumstance. The concept was then applied to family meanings and how these meanings may be constructed in the context of family disruption. The chapter also discussed some key sociological theories around the notion of family, beginning with two of the classical theories, namely, social constructionism and symbolic interactionism. The study also considered contemporary sociological concepts of family, namely, *family practices* and *family display*, which were found to be key in the understanding of family constructs by adolescents and youths living in separation from their biological families. Afrocentric theories of *Ukama* and *Ubuntu* were also discussed in relation to family meanings and values, which also provided a theoretical background for the study. These theories were discussed in reference to relevant studies that have used them, which provides an empirical base for the arguments. There is a need for more Afrocentric concepts that help to understand families in the African context, especially in light of the call to decolonise knowledge production in Africa.

REFERENCES

Abend, G. (2008). *The meaning of 'theory'. Sociological theory, 26*(2), 173–199.

Addae, E. A. (2020). The mediating role of social capital in the relationship between socioeconomic status and adolescent wellbeing: Evidence from Ghana. *BMC Public Health, 20*(1), 1–11.

Anant, S. S. (1966). Need to belong. *Canada's Mental Health, 14*(2), 21–27.

Andenæs, A. (2012). From 'placement to 'a child on the move': Methodological strategies to give children a more central position in Child Welfare Service. *Qualitative Social Work, 11*(5), 486–501.

Berger, P. L., & Luckmann, T. (1967). *The social construction of reality*. Doubleday.

Bettmann, J. E., Mortensen, J. M., & Akuoko, K. O. (2015). Orphanage caregivers' perceptions of children's emotional needs. *Children and Youth Services Review, 49*, 71–79.

Biehal, N. (2014). A sense of belonging: Meanings of family and home in long-term foster care. *British Journal of Social Work, 44*(4), 955–971.

Calheiros, M. M., Garrido, M. V., Lopes, D., & Patrício, J. N. (2015). Social images of residential care: How children, youth and residential care institutions are portrayed? *Children and Youth Services Review, 55*, 159–169.

Carsten, J. (2004). *After kinship* (Vol. 2). Cambridge University Press.

Chereni, A. (2015, May). Fathering and gender transformation in Zimbabwean transnational families. In Forum Qualitative Sozialforschung/Forum: *Qualitative Social Research*, (16), 2.

Clausen, J. A. (1966). Family structure, socialization, and personality. *Review of Child Development Research, 2*, 1–53.

Davies, H. (2011). Sharing surnames: Children, family and kinship. *Sociology, 45*(4), 554–569.

Davis, C. G., Harasymchuk, C., & Wohl, M. J. (2012). Finding meaning in a traumatic loss: A families approach. *Journal of Traumatic Stress, 25*(2), 142–149.

Després, C. (1991). The meaning of home: Literature review and directions for future research and theoretical development. *Journal of Architectural and Planning Research, 8*, 96–115.

Duncan, S., Phillips, M., Carter, J., Roseneil, S., & Stoilova, M. (2014). Practices and perceptions of living apart together. *Family Science, 5*(1), 1–10. https://doi.org/10.1080/19424620.2014.927382

Dziro, C., & Rufurwokuda, A. (2013). Post-institutional integration challenges faced by children who were raised in children's homes in Zimbabwe: The case of "ex-girl" programme for one children's home in Harare, Zimbabwe. *Greener Journal of Social Sciences, 3*(5), 268–277.

Dziro, C., Mtetwa, E., Mukamuri, B., & Chikwaiwa, B. K. (2013). Challenges faced by western-modelled residential care institutions in preparing the residents for meaningful re-integration into society: A case study of a Harare-based children's home. *Journal of Social Development in Africa, 28*(2), 113.

Erkonan, Ş. (2016). Photography and the construction of family and memory. In L. Kramp, N. Carpentier, A. Hepp, R. Kilborn, R. Kunelius, H. Nieminen, T. Olsson, P. Pruulmann-Vengerfeldt, I. T. Trivundža, & S. Tosoni (Eds.), *Politics, civil society and participation: Media and communications in a transforming environment* (pp. 257–272). edition lumière.

Erll, A. (2011). *Memory in culture*. Palgrave Macmillan.

Farmer, E., Selwyn, J., & Meakings, S. (2013). 'Other children say you're not normal because you don't live with your parents'. Children's views of living with informal kinship carers: Social networks, stigma and attachment to carers. *Child & Family Social Work, 18*(1), 25–34.

Finch, J. (2007). Displaying families. *Sociology, 41*(1), 65–81.

Finch, J. M., & Mason, J. J. (1993). *Negotiating family responsibilities*. Routledge.

Fox, A., & Berrick, J. D. (2007). A response to no one ever asked us: A review of children's experiences in out-of-home care. *Child and Adolescent Social Work Journal, 24*(1), 23–51.

Fowler, N. (2016). 'We're like one, big, dysfunctional family': Struggling to define the role of residential child care workers. *Institutionalised Children Explorations and Beyond, 3*(1), 77–90.

Furlong, A., & Cartmel, F. (2006). *Young people and social change*. McGraw-Hill Education.

Gillies, V. (2003). Family and intimate relationships: A review of the sociological research. Families & Social Capital Research Group, South Bank University.

Gubrium, J. F., & Holstein, J. A. (1993). Family discourse, organizational embeddedness, and local enactment. *Journal of Family Issues, 14*(1), 66–81.

Gwenzi, G. D. (2019). Representations of 'family' in residential care: Perspectives from residential care staff in Zimbabwe. *Scottish Journal of Residential Child Care, 18*(2), 1–15.

Hacking, I., & Hacking, J. (1999). *The social construction of what?* Harvard University Press.

Hailey, J. (2008). *Ubuntu: A literature review*. Document. London: Tutu Foundation.

Hazan, C., & Shaver, P. R. (1994). Attachment as an organizational framework for research on close relationships. *Psychological Inquiry, 5*(1), 1–22.

Hedin, L. (2014). A sense of belonging in a changeable everyday life—A follow-up study of young people in kinship, network, and traditional foster families. *Child & Family Social Work, 19*(2), 165–173.

Hess, R. D., Handel, G., & LaRossa, R. (2017). *Family worlds: A psychosocial approach to family life.* Routledge.

Hockey, J. L., & James, A. (2017). *Social identities across life course.* Macmillan International Higher Education.

Hofferth, S., & Goldscheider, F. (2016). Family heterogeneity over the life course. In *Handbook of the life course* (pp. 161–178). Springer.

Hungwe, J. P., & Ndofirepi, A. (2021). Centering "Ukama" ethic (relatedness) in the COVID-19 Pandemic 'new normal' in African higher education. *International Journal of Higher Education, 10*(5), 112–120.

Jack, G. (2015). 'I may not know who I am, but I know where I am from': The meaning of place in social work with children and families. *Child & Family Social Work, 20*(4), 415–423.

Jamieson, L. (2005). Boundaries of intimacy. In *Families in society boundaries and relationships* (pp. 188–206). https://doi.org/10.1332/policypress/9781861346438.003.0011

Jardine, C. (2017). Supporting families, promoting desistance? Exploring the impact of imprisonment on family relationships. In *New perspectives on desistance* (pp. 163–186). Palgrave Macmillan.

Jardine, C. (2018). Constructing and maintaining family in the context of imprisonment. *The British Journal of Criminology, 58*(1), 114–131.

Jones, C., & Hackett, S. (2011). The role of 'family practices' and 'displays of family' in the creation of adoptive kinship. *British Journal of Social Work, 41*(1), 40–56.

Jones, C., & Logan, J. (2013). Rediscovering family and kinship: New directions for social work theory, policy and practice. *Child and Family Social Work, 18*(1), 1–4.

Kassa, S. C. (2016). Negotiating intergenerational relationships and social expectations in childhood in rural and urban Ethiopia. *Childhood, 23*(3), 394–409.

Kauko, O., & Forsberg, H. (2018). Housing pathways, not belonging and sense of home as described by unaccompanied minors. *Nordic Social Work Research, 8*(3), 210–221.

Kendrick, A. (2013). Relations, relationships and relatedness: Residential child care and the family metaphor. *Child & Family Social Work, 18*(1), 77–86.

Kurevakwesu, W., & Maushe, F. (2020). Towards Afrocentric social work: Plotting a new path for social work theory and practice in Africa through ubuntu. *African Journal of Social Work, 10*(1), 30–35.

Lambert, N. M., Stillman, T. F., Baumeister, R. F., Fincham, F. D., Hicks, J. A., & Graham, S. M. (2010). Family as a salient source of meaning in young adulthood. *The Journal of Positive Psychology, 5*(5), 367–376.

Lappegård, T., Treas, J., Scott, J., & Richards, M. (2014). *The Wiley Blackwell companion to the sociology of families*. John Wiley & Sons.

Le Grange, L. (2012). Ubuntu, ukama and the healing of nature, self and society. *Educational Philosophy and Theory, 44*(Sup2), 56–67.

MacDonald, M. (2016). Parental entitlement and proper parenting: 'We are the parents now'. In *Parenthood and open adoption* (pp. 33–65). Palgrave Macmillan.

MacDonald, M. (2016). *Parenthood and open adoption: An interpretative phenomenological analysis*. Springer.

Mafumbate, R. (2019). The undiluted African community: Values, the family, orphanage and wellness in traditional Africa. *Information and Knowledge Management, 9*(8), 7–13.

Mason, J. (2011). What it means to be related. In V. May (Ed.), *Sociology of personal life* (pp. 59–71). Palgrave Macmillan.

McCall, R. B. (2013). The consequences of early institutionalization: Can institutions be improved? – Should they? *Child and Adolescent Mental Health, 18*(4), 193–201.

McCall, R. B., & Groark, C. J. (2015). Research on institutionalized children: Implications for international child welfare practitioners and policymakers. *International Perspectives in Psychology: Research, Practice, Consultation, 4*(2), 142.

McCormack, L., & Issaakidis, G. L. (2018). Complex trauma in childhood; psychological growth in adulthood: Making sense of the 'lived' experience of out-of-home-care. *Traumatology, 24*(2), 131.

McDaniel, S. A., & Tepperman, L. (2019). *Close relations: An introduction to the sociology of families* (6th ed.). Pearson Education Canada.

McGregor, J. (2008). Children and 'African values': Zimbabwean professionals in Britain reconfiguring family life. *Environment and Planning A, 40*(3), 596–614.

Merla, L., Nobels, B., Murru, S., & Theys, C. (2021). "Doing family" in and through space: Towards a multilocal habitus? *Recherches sociologiques et anthropologiques, 52*, 25.

Mildred, T. M. (2014). Interrogating the relevance of the extended family as a social safety net for vulnerable children in Zimbabwe. *African Journal of Social Work, 4*(2), 78–110.

Miranda, S. M., & Saunders, C. S. (2003). The social construction of meaning: An alternative perspective on information sharing. *Information Systems Research, 14*(1), 87–106.

Mlotshwa, K. (2019). Emotions of belonging and playing families across borders in Sub-Saharan Africa. In *Emotions and loneliness in a networked society* (pp. 223–238). Palgrave Macmillan.

Morgan, D. (2011). *Rethinking family practices*. Springer.

Mugumbate, J. R., & Chereni, A. (2020). Now, the theory of Ubuntu has its space in social work. *African Journal of Social Work, 10*(1), 5.

Murove, M. F. (2007). The Shona ethic of Ukama with reference to the immortality of values. *Mankind Quarterly, 48*(2), 179.

Murove, M. F. (2009). An African environmental ethic based on the concepts of ukama and ubuntu. In M. F. Murove (Ed.), *African ethics: An anthology of comparative and applied ethics*. University of Kwazulu-Natal Press.

Muzingili, T., & Gunha, P. (2017). Structural challenges of holiday placement programmes for children in SOS's children village, Zimbabwe. *African Journal of Social Work, 7*(1), 9–16.

Ndofirepi, A. P., & Shanyanana, R. N. (2016). Rethinking Ukama in the context of 'Philosophy for Children' in Africa. *Research Papers in Education, 31*(4), 428–441.

Pahl, R., & Spencer, L. (2004). Personal communities: Not simply families of 'fate' or 'choice'. *Current Sociology, 52*(2), 199–221.

Pahl, R., & Spencer, L. (2010). Family, friends, and personal communities: Changing models-in-the-mind. *Journal of Family Theory & Review, 2*(3), 197–210.

Panicker, A., Basu, K., & Chung, C. F. (2020). Changing roles and contexts: Symbolic interactionism in the sharing of food and eating practices between remote, intergenerational family members. *Proceedings of the ACM on Human-Computer Interaction, 4*(CSCW1), 1–19.

Punch, S., & McIntosh, I. (2014). 'Food is a funny thing within residential child care': Intergenerational relationships and food practices in residential care. *Childhood, 21*(1), 72–86.

Rousseau, C., Rufagari, M., Bagilishya, D., & Measham, T. (2004). Remaking family life: Strategies for re-establishing continuity among Congolese refugees during the family reunification process. *Social Science & Medicine, 59*(5), 1095–1108. https://doi.org/10.1016/j.socscimed.2003.12.011

Samuels, G. M. (2009). Ambiguous loss of home: The experience of familial (im) permanence among young adults with foster care backgrounds. *Children and Youth Services Review, 31*(12), 1229–1239.

Schutz, A. (1972). *The phenomenology of the social world*. Northwestern University Press.

Siqwana-Ndulo, N. (1998). Rural African family structure in the Eastern Cape Province, South Africa. *Journal of Comparative Family Studies, 29*(2), 407–417.

Smart, C., & Neale, B. (1999). *Family fragments?* Polity Press.

Sørensen, N. N., & Guarnizo, L. (2007). Transnational family life across the Atlantic: The experience of Colombian and Dominican migrants in Europe. In N. N. Sørensen (Ed.), *Living across worlds: Diaspora, development and transnational engagement* (pp. 151–176). International Organization for Migration.

Suter, E. A., Daas, K. L., & Bergen, K. M. (2008). Negotiating lesbian family identity via symbols and rituals. *Journal of Family Issues, 29*(1), 26–47.

Thomson, E., Winkler-Dworak, M., & Kennedy, S. (2013). The standard family life course: An assessment of variability in life course pathways. In *Negotiating the life course* (pp. 35–52). Springer.

Turney, K. (2017). Unmet health care needs among children exposed to parental incarceration. *Maternal and Child Health Journal, 21*(5), 1194–1202. https://doi.org/10.1007/s10995-016-2219-2

Waghid, Y., Van Wyk, B., Adams, F., & November, L. (2005). *African (a) philosophy of education. Reconstructions and deconstructions.* Stellenbosch University Printers, Department of Education Policy Studies (DEPS).

Wilczyńska, A., Januszek, M., & Bargiel-Matusiewicz, K. (2015). The need of belonging and sense of belonging versus effectiveness of coping. *Polish Psychological Bulletin, 46*(1), 72–81.

Wildeman, C., Turney, K., & Yi, Y. (2016). Paternal incarceration and family functioning. *The ANNALS of the American Academy of Political and Social Science, 665*(1), 80–97. https://doi.org/10.1177/0002716215625042

Winter, K., & Cohen, O. (2005). Identity issues for looked after children with no knowledge of their origins: Implications for research and practice. *Adoption & Fostering, 29*(2), 44–52.

Yi, T. H. (2019). Doing family across distance: Transnational ties and mental health among Filipina domestic workers. Retrieved May 24, 2022, from https://scholarbank.nus.edu.sg/handle/10635/158020

Zanette, D. H., & Manrubia, S. C. (2001). Vertical transmission of culture and the distribution of family names. *Physica A: Statistical Mechanics and Its Applications, 295*(1–2), 1–8.

CHAPTER 4

Constructing "Family" During Child–Family Separation

The two initial chapters of this book provided the theoretical and empirical bases for the social construction of "family" by adolescents and youths in child welfare institutions in Zimbabwe. In this chapter, the focus is now on the second crucial factor in the study, that is, the separation experience and how it may influence the construction of family meanings. It will be established how the living environment or context impacts the construction of family meanings. The question at the fore of the discussion that follows is whether separation alters family meanings. In addition, if it does, how and to what extent.

The United Nations Convention on the Rights of the Child (UNCRC, 1989) posits that every child and young person has the right to grow up in a family environment. The implication of this is that biological parents and other adult guardians (mostly kin) have the responsibility to provide family-based care for children and young people below the age of 18. However, despite the assumptions that families are close and intact, there is an overwhelming prevalence of parent–child alienation and parent–child estrangement (Scharp & Thomas, 2016). There are cases where the biological family is unwilling or unable to provide the duty of care for reasons including but not limited to parental death, loss of a job, substance abuse, parental migration, incarceration, neglect and abuse of children, and experiencing natural disasters.

G. D. Gwenzi, *Rethinking the Meaning of Family for Adolescents and Youth in Zimbabwe's Child Welfare Institutions*, Palgrave Macmillan Studies in Family and Intimate Life, https://doi.org/10.1007/978-3-031-23375-3_4

Children and young people, in this case, may experience separation from their biological families, sometimes for prolonged periods. In less developed countries, including Southern African countries, poverty has been found to be the main reason for children's separation from their families and prolonged stays in alternative care (see, e.g., Bilson & Cox, 2007; Williamson & Greenberg, 2010; Ariyadasa, 2014). Examples of separated children include unaccompanied minors, refugees, children living in the streets and institutionalised children. This book focuses on orphaned and separated children (OSC) and young people populations living in child welfare institutions. These children fall into the broader category of children without parental care (CWPC). There were an estimated 24 million children without parental care globally in 2009 (Every Child, 2009), and 2.7 million of these are living in residential forms of alternative care (UNICEF, 2021).

Child welfare interventions that result in the separation of children from their families are often accepted as necessary for the benefit and safety of the child (Raz & Sankaran, 2019). The separation of children from their families has a negative impact on their social and emotional development (Shi et al., 2021). Any rearrangement in family life has the potential to negatively impact individuals. The risk of psychopathology that stems from the separation from biological parents varies depending on the reasons leading to the separation. The negative effects of separation are also more severe when the separation is prolonged or accompanied by other forms of deprivation or victimisation (Waddoups et al., 2019). In cases of child relinquishment, defined as "a process whereby a mother and/or father or sometimes relatives with parental authority decide not to raise their child" (Bos, et al., 2015, pg. 8), the separation almost always leads to an irrevocable severance of family ties. In this case, the separation is permanent. When a relinquished child ends up in institutional care, the effects of their separation may be more profound because there is no hope of returning back to the birth family. In less frequent cases, however, there has been evidence of separation from the birth family or primary caregiver being regarded as positive. For instance, Novelle and Gonyea (2016) found evidence that some institutionalised young people managed to form new attachments in care despite the length of separation from their birth families.

THEORIES OF CHILD–FAMILY SEPARATION

Attachment Theory

Originally formulated by British psychologist John Bowlby in 1963 and further developed in 1973, attachment theory provides a foundation to understand the impact of the separation of children from their primary caregiver(s). Bowlby describes the behaviour of an infant who has experienced separation from a primary caregiver, also known as the *attachment behavioural system* (Bowlby, 1982). The attachment behavioural system refers to an "innate psychobiological system that motivates people to seek proximity to supportive others (attachment figures) in times of need" (Shaver & Mikulincer, 2012, p. 3). Separation is one of the "biologically determined signals of danger" (Baker et al., 2016, p. 177) for an infant, among other dangers, such as darkness, unfamiliar environments, being alone and being sick.

With reference to youths with a child welfare history, Stein (2006) contended that as children they may have created internal models when they experienced a disturbance in their initial attachment with a primary caregiver. The young child constructs attachment relationships that reflect their experiences with particular caregivers (Smyke et al., 2010). If they experienced rejection and loss, their internal model may reflect that loss through *attachment avoidance* and *anxiety*. The opposite is true when attachment figures are reliable and trustworthy, and a child becomes secure. However, there is evidence that suggests that children can form attachments even to abusive caregivers (Baker et al., 2016).

Bowlby indicated the need for continuity of intimate and emotional relationships between a child and their primary caregivers (Kang'ethe & Makuyan, 2014). In most institutions, especially larger ones, the caregiver–child ratio impedes emotional relationships, leading to insecure attachments among institutionalised young people. Another common feature in child welfare institutions is multiple shifts and changing caregivers, which affects attachment and emotional development (Bakermans-Kranenburg et al., 2011). Some young people experience multiple moves while in care, which may lead to attachment disconnections (Skoog et al., 2015). There is evidence that suggests that young people who have experienced disruptions in their attachment relationships may have difficulty forming and maintaining constructive and healthy relationships (see, e.g., Tomlinson et al., 2011).

Attachment theory was used to highlight the impact of separation from the biological family on adolescents' and youths' family relationships. Additionally, the potential of abuse and neglect by institutional caregivers has been noted to cause avoidant and disorganised attachment patterns that may persist throughout childhood, adolescence and adulthood (Stein, 2006).

Ambiguous Loss

Formulated by Pauline Boss (2004), ambiguous loss theory suggests that a significant individual in a person's life can be "physically absent, yet psychologically present". Boss (2004, p. 554) defined ambiguous loss as "a situation of unclear loss resulting from not knowing whether a loved one is dead or alive, absent or present". Boss described ambiguous loss as a type of grief that occurs when the loss of separation is unclear or unresolved. The grief is therefore complicated because the individual remains in the mind of those who loved them and is often unresolved. In one article, the authors explained ambiguous loss as follows:

> *When a loved one is here but not here, or gone but not for sure, the family as a whole, and the individuals in it, struggle as their story continues without an ending.* (Boss & Carnes, 2012)

Ambiguous loss theory has previously been applied to refugee youths who experienced separation from their families (e.g., Luster et al., 2009). The group of youths, who were dubbed *Lost Boys of Sudan* in the media, had been separated from their parents as early as ages six and seven, as a result of the civil war in Sudan, in the north-eastern part of Africa. Samuels (2009) applied ambiguous loss theory to understand foster children's relational losses as a result of being separated from their biological families. She conceptualised on-going losses in the family system as ambiguous loss of home.

In the Zimbabwe study, I draw from my past professional experience of working with children in a residential care facility. These young people spoke often about their birth families although they had been separated for several years. The life story sessions, which formed part of their psychotherapy, included writing memories of times spent with their mothers, fathers and other significant caregivers in their lives. Despite the negative and horrendous stories of abuse that some of them had experienced within their biological families, the latter remained a psychological figure in their lives. This further highlights the pervasive nature of the biological or blood-related family and how in some cultures, particularly the African culture, the bond persists even in bad or abusive circumstances. In retrospect, the young people I encountered in practice maintained complex emotional ties with their biological families and "mourned'' their loss; however, most times, it remained unresolved due to the prolonged time they spent in care. In particular, some young people who had experienced abandonment at infancy verbalised an idealised view of their birth families, even in the context of separation. Additionally, young people who had lost contact with their birth families held on to the hope that one day they would return. Using this past experience, the academic curiosity to examine how young people in Zimbabwe's child welfare institutions would make sense of "family" in the context of biological family separation was born.

SEPARATION AND PLACEMENT IN INSTITUTIONAL CARE

Institution-reared children experience separation from or loss of their birth parents and other caregivers (van IJzendoorn et al., 2011). This may be brief or for prolonged periods of time. Placement in institutional care often means prolonged separation from the biological family and community of origin. In Zimbabwe and other Southern African countries, institutionalisation undermines the traditional models of care for children and young people and alienates them from their families, communities and cultures (Masuka et al., 2012). What often makes the separation experience worse is that in countries such as Zimbabwe, children are often placed in institutions far removed from their familiar surroundings and communities. Furthermore, children exposed to institutional care, in most cases, do not receive the type of nurturing and stimulating environment needed for healthy psychological development (Bakermans-Kranenburg et al., 2011). However, even for children who had relatively secure attachments prior to the separation, the experience of being separated from home even temporarily into institutional care has a huge impact on children's emotional well-being and sense of self (Ward, 2004).

The timing of separation from the birth family is a crucial factor when considering its impact. Child–family separation, especially in the early years, leads to long-term feelings of abandonment and attachment issues (Smyke et al., 2010). There exists documented evidence that childhood disadvantage and adverse childhood experiences (ACES), including family breakdown and separation, have long-reaching effects into adulthood, forming a cycle of poverty and disadvantage (Stark et al., 2014). For instance, evidence of teenage pregnancy in care leavers has been predicted by previous circumstances such as sexual abuse (Barn & Mantovani, 2006), limited sex education before coming into care (Vinnerljung et al., 2007) and the pursuit of a sense of belonging (Connolly et al., 2012).

Other studies have also found that institutional care leavers may develop feelings of self-blame and rejection (Schofield et al., 2017) continuing into adulthood due to their childhood circumstances. Furthermore, the predominantly negative experiences faced by children who have been separated from their birth families may be a contributing factor in their understanding of family. Because of the early circumstances of most children in institutions, including abuse, neglect, abandonment and other adverse experiences in their birth families, it is not surprising that their constructions of "family" may be complex.

One may question why institutional care is still being used, particularly in sub-Saharan Africa, despite the evidence of its unsuitability for children's optimum development. From my analysis and research, in most sub-Saharan African countries, alternative care forms such as foster care by non-relatives and adoption are not as common because they are considered culturally unviable (Subbarao & Coury, 2004; Tembo & Oltedal, 2015). In Zimbabwe, for instance, families fear the passing of generational curses if they foster or adopt an unrelated child (Powell et al., 2004). Similarly, in Nigeria, community members feel that adoption contravenes societal and cultural conventions to adopt because it has not been done before in their community (Adewunmi et al., 2012). This leaves residential/institutional forms of alternative care as the only viable option available to children without adequate care and children without parental care. However, scholars maintain that even in instances where community-based approaches are not available, community forms of care would still be preferable compared to placing OVCs in institutional care (Chikwaiwa et al., 2013).

On the other hand, some scholars argue that institutional forms of care benefit some children (e.g., Khang'ethe & Nyamutinga, 2014; Novelle & Gonyea, 2016; Whetten et al., 2009, 2014), stating that some children do fare better in institutions than in family care, particularly in cases of extreme abuse, disability and deprivation. In some cases, OVC institutions reduce government pressure to provide adequate social and welfare support to vulnerable children living with their families (Kang'ethe & Nyamutinga, 2014).

Taking a further look into the unique features of institutional care that make it undesirable and having predominantly negative outcomes, one contentious issue has been the question of whether the state, which is responsible for the care of children without adequate parental or family care, can actually function as a corporate parent (Bullock et al., 2006). The idea of a corporate parent in the form of government agencies has fallen under criticism because the duty of caring for children becomes invested in corporate organisations rather than private individuals (Bullock et al., 2006). Parental responsibilities often require more personal and close relationships; however, some studies find that full responsibility and parental rights are rarely assigned to the children's caregivers in institutions (e.g., Darkwah, Daniel & Yendork, 2018).

Extrafamilial Care

Also described as out-of-home care, extrafamilial care is a temporary, medium- or long-term living arrangement for children and young people who cannot live or be cared for in their nuclear family home. The first unique characteristic of institutional care is extrafamilial group care. Growing up in a child welfare institution exposes young people to a different kind of upbringing and a different socialisation compared to children growing up in their birth families. Each group home has its own culture (Anglin, 2002) that children are socialised into when they become residents. The ethos of institutional shelters is to provide the child and adolescent with reception, care and a space for socialisation and development, offering the possibility of a positive and stable relationship with a caregiver (Donato et al., 2017). However, the child welfare institution remains a public institutional arrangement that, to a larger extent, reflects a public rather than private life, particularly when it is a dormitory-style and not a family-style model. This implies that the extrafamilial group living, in most cases, is found to be lacking in terms of being a "home". No matter how much a group home attempts to create a family environment and a sense of family life, the young people living in those settings are always aware that it is not "normal" for them to grow up there. In addition, most institutions can only offer care during the child's residency (Carlson, 2015); once the child reaches the age of majority (18), they are expected to leave. This temporal nature of residential care placement deters young people from feeling completely "at home" and forming lasting relationships with individuals in that setting. Furthermore, as Tolfree (2003) states, in the vast majority of cases, institutional care involves large numbers of children living in an artificial setting, which effectively detaches them not only from their own immediate and extended family and from their community of origin but also from meaningful interaction with the community in which the institution is located.

Involvement of the Birth Family

The everyday lives of children in substitute care are influenced by child welfare policy and practices related to the involvement of the birth family (Boddy, et al., 2013). This is because the birth family still exists for most adolescents and youths living in child welfare institutions, with studies stating that 60–90% of children in institutions have at least one surviving parent and relatives (Bunkers et al., 2014). In 2008, close to 90% of orphans in Southern African countries were being cared for by traditional family networks (Lombe & Ochumbo, 2008), including the extended family. The influence of the birth family, at least in the Southern African context, was strong at this time; however, as noted previously, the capacity of families to care for their children has been severely compromised. Zimbabwe has been reported to be doing very little in terms of preventing child–family separation (CRINSA & World Vision International, 2018).

Contact is one of the ways through which the birth family becomes involved with young people in child welfare institutions. Contact has been defined as any direct or indirect communication between a child and significant others, ranging from an exchange of letters or emails, swapping photographs, telephone calls and infrequent supervised visits to infrequent or frequent meetings that may or may not be supervised (Taplin, 2005, p.1). Contact is often something that coresident individuals take for granted; however, for those living in separation, contact can make a huge difference, as it is a crucial component to maintaining social connectedness and relationships. Contact between looked-after young people and their birth families is often associated with positive outcomes, but it is also a contentious issue (Sen & Broadhurst, 2011). Well-managed contact is said to improve the chances of family reunification and provides young people with a greater sense of their origins and identity (Taplin & Mattick, 2013).

Research by Sen and Broadhurst (2011) in the United Kingdom showed that contact is necessary for family reunification. Contact, even occasional, can keep a child's sense of their origins alive and may offer future networks of support for care leavers given that a large proportion of children will return to their birth families at some point in their lives (Sen & Broadhurst, 2011). However, this is not always a linear or simple process. Children in care may differentiate between family members and may want contact with particular family members but not others. Contact with the birth family also depends on the circumstances that led to the child's removal from their familial home. There are also several complications within the child welfare system, particularly in the Zimbabwean context, that make contact impossible or less frequent. These include a lack of human resources to supervise contact between children and birth families and a lack of financial resources for the birth families to continue travelling to the child welfare institution,[1] just to name a few. In Malawi, there were also reports of limited contact between young people in institutions and their biological families (UNICEF Malawi, 2011). However, except in cases of severe child abuse and neglect, contact is usually encouraged to maintain young people's psychological identity and well-being. In instances, when children are separated from their birth families as infants, for example, abandoned or relinquished children, contact might not be an option.

One distinctive feature of contact for young people in child welfare institutions is that their contact with their birth family or guardians is often supervised. Supervised contact refers to contact in which interaction and conversation between the parent and child are closely monitored at a specialist contact centre and notes are taken by the person accompanying the child, usually a social worker provided by the court or child protection services (Bullen et al., 2015). In the United States, it is a best practice that the first visit after a child has been removed from their birth family must be supervised for the purposes of child protection. Children's legislation in most countries specifies the frequency and duration of family contact for children in out-of-home care.

In Zimbabwe, the Children's Protection Act (Chapter 5:06) does not make clear provisions for visitation procedures by family members while a child is in the child welfare institution. One disturbing report from a study

---

[1] Most young people are placed in institutions that are located far away from their community of origin, which would necessitate travel in order to see each other.

conducted in Masvingo Province of Zimbabwe stated that children's relatives are not allowed to visit because they feel that they might be forced to take the child back home with them (Mupfumira et al., 2013). This may be explained by the context of poverty, where relatives would rather be separated from their children if they are not able to care for them. However, for young people who are placed in institutions, feelings of abandonment and rejection are commonplace, especially if visits never take place while they are in the institution. This goes against Article 9 of the UNCRC (1989), which stipulates the rights of children who are separated from their parents to maintain personal relations and direct contact with both parents on a regular basis, except if it is contrary to the child's best interests. In instances where there is a history of maltreatment or the family is still struggling with substance abuse issues, unsupervised contact may lead to emotional harm and may disrupt the child's development (Sen & Broadhurst, 2011).

The study by Mupfumira et al. (2013) in Zimbabwe also noted that children were allowed to visit only those homes that were vetted by the Social Welfare officers if they were abused. While this is commendable, it highlights a flaw in social service monitoring and family reconstructive services for families whose children have been removed. Instead of continuing the separation of children from their families under the guise of protecting them from abuse, perhaps the Department of Social Welfare (DSW) should emphasise preventative interventions and work with families that have abused children to get the help that they require. There is a severe shortage of these kinds of services in Zimbabwe due to an incapacitated social workforce.

Relationships with Caregivers in the Institution

The relationships between young people in child welfare institutions and their caregivers must follow certain professional regulations and are, therefore, not organic. There have also been reports of young people being abused in institutions (e.g., Browne, 2009; Martin & Sudrajat, 2007). The relationship between young people and their caregivers has been associated with ambiguity and confusion. For instance, in the United Kingdom, due to the scandals of abuse in residential care, there has been a distancing of the professional relationship, with concerns about touch and physical contact (Steckley & Smith, 2011).

Most young people in child welfare institutions also do not trust the child welfare system (Newton et al., 2022) due to systemic abuses and maltreatment (Uliando & Mellor, 2012). The use of physical and psychological punishment was prevalent in many institutions in Indonesia (Martin & Sudrajat, 2007). Poorly trained residential staff have been attributed to the harmful practices found in most institutions (SOS Children's Villages, 2014). Additionally, children living in institutional care also suffer from structural neglect, which may include minimum physical resources, unfavourable and unstable staffing patterns, and socially emotionally inadequate caregiver–child interactions.

Young people in child welfare institutions not only are separated from their birth families and placed with unrelated caregivers, but also experience, as part of their day-to-day lived experience, multiple relationships with other individuals. Institutional care relationships often include interactions with the child welfare system (social workers and child care workers) and the justice system (Children's Court) responsible for legalising the removal of children from their legal guardians. Figure 4.1 illustrates some of these multiple relationships that adolescents and youths in

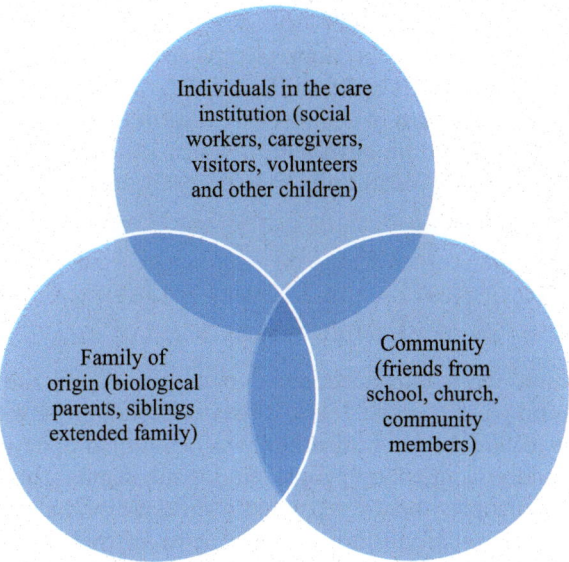

Fig. 4.1 Multifaceted relationships in child care institutions. Source: Authors' own

institutions may be exposed to. Studies have found that the child's birth parents often feel excluded from decision-making about their children when they are in the institution (Berrick et al., 2016). This implies that the child welfare and judiciary are usually at the forefront of decision-making about children in institutions, which is different from when the child lives with their birth family. This is bound to affect the child's relationship with the birth family.

Young people in the child welfare institution are expected to navigate and make sense of these multiple relationships on a daily basis, and it is a wonder that the complexity of the emotions this evokes has been largely ignored, particularly in Zimbabwe and the Southern African region. Most of the relationships are transient, leaving young people with a sense of loss and feelings of rejection. In fact, Driscoll (2018) examined the effect of living with strangers as well as transient relationships with caregiver professionals on residential care leavers in England and found evidence of loss, separation and feelings of rejection. Unfortunately, in the context of Zimbabwe, the impact of multiple relationships in alternative care has not yet been documented.

Given this background on the features of the child welfare institution and its impact on young people, Sng (2009, p. 249) warns that for many children in care, the term family may carry some "inescapable negative connotations of abandonment, unpredictability and pain". Young people may feel anger and resentment towards their biological families for exposing them to the conditions in child welfare institutions. Granted this view romanticises life within the birth family, which is not the case in reality. However, child welfare institutions have always been compared to family life in a negative way.

Constructing Family Meanings During Child–Family Separation

The subchapter above introduced child–family separation and its impact on children and young people. It also discussed separation and subsequent placement in a child welfare institution, which is argued to have a negative impact on children and young people. In this subchapter, the focus turns to how young people who are separated from their biological family and placed in a child welfare institution make sense of their family relationships. In other words, how do young people construct the meaning of family in the context of biological family separation and subsequent placement in a child welfare institution?

The child welfare institution, in this case, is considered the context in which adolescents and youths are constructing their meanings of family after their family has been disrupted or has malfunctioned in some way. Boddy (2019) notes that the concept of family in residential care is instrumentalised through the language of contact, reunification and permanence (Boddy, 2019). Contact is described as a direct (face-to-face) or indirect (telephone calls, letters) interaction with the biological family after separation has occurred (Collings et al., 2018). Reunification describes attempts to return the child or young person back to their family. As described earlier, there is a relationship between contact and reunification in that children who experience regular contact during separation are more likely to be reunified with their biological families (Sen & Broadhurst, 2011). Legal permanence is defined as the reunification, adoption or transfer of legal guardianship of youth and remains a critical goal to achieve for youth in child welfare systems (Brown et al., 2006). Permanence becomes necessary when there is no option to return to the biological family, either because their conditions may have worsened and the environment is not safe to return to, or because they are unwilling or unable to take the child or young person back in. These three concepts, contact, reunification and permanence, influence how the meaning of family may be constructed by young people. Because birth families are often psychologically present in the minds of children during separation (Boddy et al., 2013), family meanings of young people living in separation tend to be complex.

It is also crucial when thinking about family disruption and separation to consider the goals of child welfare after separation from the biological family has occurred. In the first instance, the initial goal of placement in a child welfare institution is usually to protect the child or young person. The second goal, ideally, should be interventions towards family continuity and reconstruction to solve the issues that necessitate the removal of the child/young person. In the case that these issues are not resolved, they continue into adulthood, impacting the lives of young people. Considering the child welfare system in Zimbabwe and most Southern African countries, family reconstructive services are lacking, mostly due to scarce human and financial resources to conduct home visits. This implies that young people can be placed in child welfare institutions for prolonged periods with no contact with their birth families or efforts made to reconstruct their families to ensure their safe return. The familial relationships may also remain strained for several years in the absence of therapeutic interventions and family support services. In this case, family belonging may need to be reconstructed repeatedly (Stoilova et al., 2017).

It is hypothesised that adolescents and youths will also have complex views of their family relationships due to their experiences with their biological family prior to their removal. For instance, young people who experienced abuse or neglect by the biological family may need time to process what happened to them and may not be so willing to reconnect with their birth families or rebuild the broken relationships (Watson et al. 2021). However, as noted earlier, it is possible for abused and/or maltreated children to still form attachments with their parents or caregivers. In addition, the nature of young people's relationships with both the birth family and the unrelated individuals in the child welfare institution adds confusion to their constructions of family. Indeed, studies of youths who have grown up in the child welfare system and exited the care system (care leavers) have found evidence of care leavers struggling with making sense of their family relationships and troubled relationships with the family of origin (see, e.g., Bengtsson et al. (2020); Boddy, 2019; Enell & Wilińska, 2021; Gwenzi, 2020). The experience of being institutionalised, coupled with challenging relationships with the birth family, and the transition from care to adulthood, often in the absence of the birth family, further complicate care leavers' family meanings (Sting & Groinig, 2020).

CONCLUSION

Child–family separation has an impact on how children and youths construct the meanings of family. The timing of separation and the age at which a young person is separated also influence how they respond to the separation and how they respond to their caregivers. The subsequent placement in a child welfare institution also introduces new dynamics, including extrafamilial care, relationships with non-kin individuals and, in some cases, continued contact with the biological family. These dynamics will have an impact on how family meanings are constructed during separation. According to the ambiguous loss theory, during separation, the biological family remains psychologically present, although physically absent. This complicates young people's views about their families because in most cases, their issues with their families remain unresolved. Young people form attachments to their biological families as their immediate caregivers, and when these attachments are disrupted, how family relationships are viewed often becomes distorted. In the child welfare institution, new relationships are also formed that may or may not lead to new attachments. However, in most cases, the transient nature of relationships in care impedes the formation of long-lasting bonds. Furthermore, while in the child welfare institution, young people may experience contact with the biological family or a lack thereof, which will also determine their meanings of family. Contact may speed up the reunification process as familial relationships are maintained through interaction.

REFERENCES

Adewunmi, A. A., Tayo, A. O., Rabiu, K. A., Akindele, R. A., Ottun, T. A., & Akinlusi, F. M. (2012). Factors associated with acceptability of child adoption as a management option for infertility among women in a developing country. *International Journal of Women's Health*, 365. https://doi.org/10.2147/ijwh.s31598

Anglin, J. P. (2002). *Staffed Group homes for children and youth: Constructing a theoretical framework for understanding*. Doctoral dissertation, University of Leicester. https://figshare.com/articles/thesis/Staffed_Group_Homes_for_Children_and_Youth_Constructing_a_Theoretical_Framework_for_Understanding/10099838

Ariyadasa, E. (2014). Poverty and perception: Driving Sri Lankan children's homes at multiple levels. Retrieved April 10, 2022, from http://ir.kdu.ac.lk/bitstream/handle/345/1595/mgt010.pdf?sequence=1&isAllowed=y

Baker, A. J., Creegan, A., Quinones, A., & Rozelle, L. (2016). Foster children's views of their birth parents: A review of the literature. *Children and Youth Services Review*, 67, 177–183.

Bakermans-Kranenburg, M. J., Steele, H., Zeanah, C. H., Muhamedrahimov, R. J., Vorria, P., Dobrova-Krol, N. A., et al. (2011). III. Attachment and emotional development in institutional care: Characteristics and catch up. *Monographs of the Society for Research in Child Development*, 76(4), 62–91.

Barn, R., & Mantovani, N. (2006). Young mothers and the care system: Contextualizing risk and vulnerability. *British Journal of Social Work*, 37(2), 225–243. https://doi.org/10.1093/bjsw/bcl002

Bengtsson, M., Sjöblom, Y., & Öberg, P. (2020). Transitional patterns when leaving care—Care leavers' agency in a longitudinal perspective. *Children and Youth Services Review*, 118, 105486.

Berrick, J., Dickens, J., Pösö, T., & Skivenes, M. (2016). Time, institutional support, and quality of decision making in child protection: A cross-country analysis. *Human Service Organizations: Management, Leadership & Governance*, 40(5), 451–468.

Bilson, A., & Cox, P. (2007). Caring about poverty: Alternatives to institutional care for children in poverty. *Journal of Children and Poverty*, 13(1), 37–55.

Boddy, J. (2019). Troubling meanings of "family" for young people who have been in care: From policy to lived experience. *Journal of Family Issues*, 40(16), 2239–2263.

Boddy, J., Statham, J., Danielsen, I., Geurts, E., Join-Lambert, H., & Euillet, S. (2013). Beyond contact: Work with families of children placed away from home in four European countries. Brighton: University of Sussex, Centre for Innovation and Research in Childhood and Youth.

Boddy, J., Statham, J., Danielsen, I., Geurts, E., Join-Lambert, H., & Euillet, S. (2013). *Beyond contact. Work with families of children placed away from home in four European countries.* University of Sussex.

Bos, K., Zeanah, C. H., Fox, N. A., Drury, S. S., McLaughlin, K. A., & Nelson, C. A. (2011). Psychiatric outcomes in young children with a history of institutionalization. *Harvard Review of Psychiatry, 19*(1), 15–24.

Boss, P. (2004). Ambiguous loss research, theory, and practice: Reflections after 9/11. *Journal of Marriage and Family, 66*(3), 551–566.

Boss, P., & Carnes, D. (2012). The myth of closure. *Family Process, 51*(4), 456–469.

Bowlby, J. (1982). Attachment and loss: Retrospect and prospect. *American Journal of Orthopsychiatry, 52*(4), 664.

Brown, I., Léveillé, S., & Gough, P. (2006). Is permanence necessary for resilience? Advice for policy makers. *Promoting Resilience in Child Welfare*, 94–115.

Browne, K. (2009). The risk of harm to young children in institutional care. London: Save the Children. https://bettercarenetwork.org/library/particular-threats-to-childrens-care-and-protection/effects-of-institutional-care/the-risk-of-harm-to-youngpeople-in-institutional-care

Bullen, T., Taplin, S., & Barry, E. (2015). Supporting quality contact visits for children in out-of-home care. Institute of Child Protection Studies Research to Practice Series. https://doi.org/10.24268/fhs.8343

Bullock, R., Courtney, M. E., Parker, R., Sinclair, I., & Thoburn, J. (2006). Can the corporate state parent? *Adoption & Fostering, 30*(4), 6–19.

Bunkers, K., Cox, A., Gesiriech, S., & Olson, K. (2014). Children, orphanages, and families: A summary of research to help guide faith-based action. Retrieved August 25, 2019, from https://bettercarenetwork.org/library/the-continuum-of-care/residential-care/children-orphanages-and-families-a-summary-of-research-to-help-guidefaith-based-action

Carlson, R. (2015). A child's right to a family versus a state's right to institutionalize the child. *Journal of International Law, 47*(3), 2016. Retrieved May 6, 2019, from https://ssrn.com/abstract=2653837

Chikwaiwa, B. K., Nyikahadzoi, K., Matsika, A. B., & Dziro, C. (2013). Factors that enhance intrapersonal wellness of orphans and other vulnerable children (OVC) in institutions and community-based settings in Zimbabwe. *Journal of Social Development in Africa, 28*(2), 53.

Child Rights Network for Southern Africa (CRINSA) & World Vision International. (2018). Measuring government efforts to protect girls and boys—Zimbabwe Child Rights Barometer. Retrieved March 31, 2022, from https://reliefweb.int/sites/reliefweb.int/files/resources/Child%20rights%20barometer%20-%20Zimbabwe%202018%20-%20Measuring%20government%20efforts%20to%20protect%20girls%20and%20boys.pdf

Collings, S., Neil, E., & Wright, A. C. (2018). Practices to improve communication between birth parents and permanent families. *Advances in Social Work and Welfare Education, 20*(2), 144–150.

Connolly, J., Heifetz, M., & Bohr, Y. (2012). Pregnancy and motherhood among adolescent girls in child protective services: A meta-synthesis of qualitative research. *Journal of Public Child Welfare, 6*(5), 614–635.

Darkwah, E., Daniel, M., & Yendork, J. S. (2018). Care-'less': Exploring the interface between child care and parental control in the context of child rights for workers in children's homes in Ghana. *BMC International Health and Human Rights, 18*, 1–12.

Donato, L. D. J. F. C., Magalhaes, C. M. C., & da Silva Corrêa, L. (2017). Practices of care from educators at institutional shelters for children. *Psychology, 8*(08), 1161.

Driscoll, J. J. (2018). *Reconceptualising transitions from care to independence: Supporting care leavers to fulfil their potential.* Routledge.

Enell, S., & Wilińska, M. (2021). "My whole family is not really my family"—Secure care shadows on family and family practices among young adults and their family members. *Journal of Family Issues.* https://doi.org/10.1177/0192513X211030026

Every Child. (2009). Missing: Children without parental care in international development policy. Retrieved August 23, 2022, from https://bettercarenetwork.org/library/social-welfare-systems/child-care-and-protection-policies/missing-children-without-parental-care-in-international-development-policy

Gwenzi, G. D. (2020). Constructing the meaning of "family" in the context of out-of-home care: An exploratory study on residential care leavers in Harare, Zimbabwe. *Emerging Adulthood, 8*(1), 54–63.

Kang'ethe, S. M., & Nyamutinga, D. (2014). The panacea and perfidy associated with Orphaned and Vulnerable Children (OVCs) living in institutionalized care in some countries of the developing world. *Journal of Social Sciences, 41*(2), 117–124.

Kang'ethe, S. M., & Makuyan, A. (2014). Orphans and vulnerable children (OVC) care institutions: Exploring their possible damage to children in a few countries of the developing world. *Journal of Social Sciences, 38*(2), 117–124.

Lombe, M., & Ochumbo, A. (2008). Sub-Saharan Africa's orphan crisis: Challenges and opportunities. *International Social Work, 51*(5), 682–698.

Luster, T., Qin, D., Bates, L., Johnson, D., & Rana, M. (2009). The lost boys of Sudan: Coping with ambiguous loss and separation from parents. *American Journal of Orthopsychiatry, 79*(2), 203–211.

Martin, F., & Sudrajat, T. (2007). Someone that matters: The quality of care in childcare institutions in Indonesia. Jakarta: Save the Children UK/The Ministry of Social Affairs (DEPSOS)/UNICEF. Retrieved August 23, 2022, from http://bettercarenetwork.org/library/social-welfare-systems/child-care-andprotection-system-reforms/indonesia-changing-the-paradigm-save-thechildren%C2%80%C2%99s-work-to-strengthen-the-child-protection-system

Masuka, T., Banda, R. G., Mabvurira, V., & Frank, R. (2012). Preserving the future: Social protection programmes for orphans and vulnerable children (OVC) in Zimbabwe. Centre for Promoting Ideas, USA.

Mupfumira, I. M., Madungwe, L. S., & Chindedza, W. (2013). Children's homes: A refuge for vulnerable children in society: A case study of a children's home in Masvingo Province in Zimbabwe.

Novelle, M. A., & Gonyea, J. G. (2016). The availability and role of non-parental identity agents for institutionalized male adolescent social orphans in Colombia: Child and youth services review. *Children and Youth Services Review, 61,* 51–60.

Powell, G., Chinake, T., Mudzinge, D., Maambira, W., Mukutiri, S., & UNICEF. (2004). Children in residential care: The Zimbabwean experience. Retrieved August 28, 2018, from https://bettercarenetwork.org/library/the-continuum-of-care/residential-care/children-in-residential-care-thezimbabwean-experience

Raz, M., & Sankaran, V. (2019). Opposing family separation policies for the welfare of children. *American Journal of Public Health, 109*(11), 1529.

Samuels, G. M. (2009). Ambiguous loss of home: The experience of familial (im) permanence among young adults with foster care backgrounds. *Children and Youth Services Review, 31*(12), 1229–1239.

Scharp, K. M., & Thomas, L. J. (2016). Family "bonds": Making meaning of parent–child relationships in estrangement narratives. *Journal of Family Communication, 16*(1), 32–50.

Schofield, G., Larsson, B., & Ward, E. (2017). Risk, resilience and identity construction in the life narratives of young people leaving residential care. *Child & Family Social Work, 22*(2), 782–791.

Sen, R., & Broadhurst, K. (2011). Contact between children in out-of-home placements and their family and friends networks: A research review. *Child & Family Social Work, 16*(3), 298–309.

Shaver, P. R., & Mikulincer, M. (2012). An attachment perspective on coping with existential concerns. In P. R. Shaver & M. Mikulincer (Eds.), *Meaning, mortality, and choice: The social psychology of existential concerns* (pp. 291–307). American Psychological Association.

Shi, H., Wang, Y., Li, M., Tan, C., Zhao, C., Huang, X., et al. (2021). Impact of parent-child separation on children's social-emotional development: A cross-sectional study of left-behind children in poor rural areas of China. *BMC Public Health, 21*(1), 1–10.

Skoog, V., Khoo, E., & Nygren, L. (2015). Disconnection and dislocation: Relationships and belonging in unstable foster and institutional care. *The British Journal of Social Work, 45*(6), 1888–1904.

Smyke, A. T., Zeanah, C. H., Fox, N. A., Nelson, C. A., & Guthrie, D. (2010). Placement in foster care enhances quality of attachment among young institutionalized children. *Child Development, 81*(1), 212–223.

Sng, R. (2009). Family therapy for kids without families: Working systemically with children and young people in residential care. *Australian and New Zealand Journal of Family Therapy, 30*(4), 247–259.

SOS Children's Villages International. (2014). Assessment Report of the Alternative Care System for Children in Zimbabwe. Retrieved from SOS Zimbabwe Website on February 15, 2017, from https://www.soschildrensvillages.org/getmedia/eeaf524d-4486-4aaf-b786-ea44b3c11295/Zimbabwe-small.pdf

Stark, L., Rubenstein, B. L., Muldoon, K., & Roberts, L. (2014). *Guidelines for implementing a national strategy to determine the magnitude and distribution of children outside of family care.* Center for Excellence on Children in Adversity.

Steckley, L., & Smith, M. (2011). Care ethics in residential child care: A different voice. *Ethics and Social Welfare, 5*(2), 181–195.

Stein, M. (2006). Young people aging out of care: The poverty of theory. *Children and Youth Services Review, 28*(4), 422–434.

Sting, S., & Groinig, M. (2020). Care leavers' perspectives on the family in the transition from out-of-home care to independent living. *International Journal of Child, Youth and Family Studies, 11*(4), 140–159.

Stoilova, M., Roseneil, S., Carter, J., Duncan, S., & Phillips, M. (2017). Constructions, reconstructions and deconstructions of 'family' amongst people who live apart together (LATs). *The British Journal of Sociology, 68*(1), 78–96.

Subbarao, K., & Coury, D. (2004). *Reaching out to Africa's orphans: A framework for public action.* World Bank Publications.

Taplin, S. (2005). Is all contact between children in care and their birth parents' good' contact?: Discussion Paper. NSW Centre for Parenting & Research, Department of Community Services.

Taplin, S., & Mattick, R. P. (2013). Mothers in methadone treatment and their involvement with the child protection system: A replication and extension study. *Child Abuse & Neglect, 37*(8), 500–510. https://doi.org/10.1016/j.chiabu.2013.01.003

Tembo, M. J., & Oltedal, S. (2015). Social work and families in child welfare in Malawi: Social workers considerations when placing a child outside the home. *Journal of Comparative Social Work.* https://doi.org/10.31265/jcsw.v10i1.122

Tolfree, D. (2003). Community based care for separated children. Stockholm: Save the children Sweden. Retrieved August 2, 2017, from https://better-carenetwork.org/sites/default/files/Community%20Based%20Care%20for%20Separated%20Children.pdf

Tomlinson, P., Gonzalez, R., & Barton, S. (2011). *Therapeutic residential care for children and young people: An attachment and trauma-informed model for practice.* Jessica Kingsley Publishers.

Uliando, A., & Mellor, D. (2012). Maltreatment of children in out-of-home care: A review of associated factors and outcomes. *Children and Youth Services Review, 34*(12), 2280–2286.

UNCRC. (1989). United Nations Convention on the Rights of the Child. Retrieved May 25, 2022, from https://www.unicef.org.uk/wp-content/uploads/2010/05/UNCRC_united_nations_convention_on_the_rights_of_the_child.pdf

UNICEF. (2021). Children without parental care. Retrieved August 10, 2022, from https://www.unicef.org/topics/children-without-parental-care

UNICEF Malawi. (2011). The Ministry of Gender, Children, and Community Development of Malawi; Centre for Social Research (CSR) of the University of Malawi. Retrieved May 25, 2022, from http://www.bettercarenetwork.org/library/the-continuum-of-care/residential-care/all-children-count-a-baseline-study-of-children-in-institutional-care-in-malawi

Van IJzendoorn, M. H., Palacios, J., Sonuga-Barke, E. J., Gunnar, M. R., Vorria, P., McCall, R. B., et al. (2011). Children in institutional care: Delayed development and resilience. *Monographs of the Society for Research in Child Development, 76*(4), 8–30.

Vinnerljung, B., Franzén, E., & Danielsson, M. (2007). Teenage parenthood among child welfare clients: A Swedish national cohort study of prevalence and odds. *Journal of Adolescence, 30*(1), 97–116. https://doi.org/10.1016/j.adolescence.2005.12.002

Waddoups, A. B., Yoshikawa, H., & Strouf, K. (2019). Developmental effects of parent–child separation. *Annual Review of Developmental Psychology, 1*, 387–410.

Ward, H. (2004). Working with managers to improve services: Changes in the role of research in social care. *Child & Family Social Work, 9*(1), 13–25.

Watson, D. L., Staples, E., & Riches, K. (2021). 'We need to understand what's going on because it's our life': Using sandboxing to understand children and young people's everyday conversations about care. *Children & Society, 35*(5), 663–679.

Whetten, K., Ostermann, J., Pence, B. W., Whetten, R. A., Messer, L. C., Ariely, S., et al. (2014). Three-year change in the wellbeing of orphaned and separated children in institutional and family-based care settings in five low- and middle-income countries. *PLoS ONE, 9*(8). https://doi.org/10.1371/journal.pone.0104872

Whetten, K., Ostermann, J., Whetten, R. A., Pence, B. W., O'Donnell, K., Messer, L. C., & Thielman, N. M. (2009). A comparison of the wellbeing of orphans and abandoned children ages 6–12 in institutional and community-based care settings in 5 less wealthy nations. *PLoS ONE, 4*(12). https://doi.org/10.1371/journal.pone.0008169

Williamson, J., & Greenberg, A. (2010). Families, not orphanages. Retrieved December 25, 2014, from https://bettercarenetwork.org/library/particular-threats-to-childrens-care-and-protection/effects-of-institutional-care/families-not-orphanage

CHAPTER 5

Family in Southern Africa

As a starting point, families in sub-Saharan Africa have long been extraordinarily diverse and complex (Gabrielli et al., 2018). Furthermore, the importance of the family as a unit of production, consumption, reproduction and accumulation has been well documented. Traditionally, family forms in this region were heterogeneous in their form, structure, function and evolution (Sooryamoorthy & Chetty, 2015). Most foundational ethnographies on kinship were conducted in West, East and Southern Africa because of this diversity of family structures. African families were built on patrilineal, matrilineal or bilateral lineage patterns and coresidential or non-coresidential polygamy that did not conform to "western" categories (Gage, 1997). In particular, the extended family predominated over the nuclear family, which largely distinguished the conception and the organisation of the Southern African family from the Western family. Marriage was viewed as a worthy and serious commitment, a covenant between two (extended) families, kindred and villages. Concepts of family then included the idea of "living together" and the sense of "community of brothers and sisters" as the basis of, and the expression of, the extended family system in Africa (Mafumbate, 2019).

Families in Zimbabwe are constructed in the same way families in Southern Africa have always been, mainly from patrilineal descent

G. D. Gwenzi, *Rethinking the Meaning of Family for Adolescents and Youth in Zimbabwe's Child Welfare Institutions*, Palgrave Macmillan Studies in Family and Intimate Life, https://doi.org/10.1007/978-3-031-23375-3_5

(Russell, 2004). The father's side of the family was and is still said to be the origin of each individual. Family meanings were symbolised through kinship, which is a persistent and important relationship. In rural areas, the family unit is composed of the husband, the wife or wives, children and members of the extended family. In urban areas, households are smaller, with a tendency towards a nuclear family of the husband, the wife, and children. There are also polygynous families, where each wife has her own house and a portion of a field. This is often found among wealthier tribes. Households are usually defined in terms of a domestic unit of the wife, the children and other dependents; therefore, a polygynous family and a wider extended family living together may consist of two or more households. The average household size in Zimbabwe as of 2022 by province is approximately 4.0 persons (ZimStat, 2022).

Descent-based kinship is not confined to a residual, intimate, domestic sphere, but it has been the basis for the day-to-day organisation of production and for the distribution of authority in the African community (Russell, 2004). Kinship was and still is the organising principle in African societies, including Zimbabwe. Kin today can still be found in their groups performing events such as funerals and family celebrations such as weddings. Kinship is also represented, for instance, through the practice of totemism, where an individual takes the totem of their patrilineal tribe at birth. Totemism is a cultural practice used to identify the different clans among the Shona people in Zimbabwe, and historically, they made up the dynasties of the ancient tribes. The totems came from certain traits displayed by the tribe's ancestor; for example, if he showed great strength, he was viewed as a lion and thus given the totem "lion", and all his descendants would take the same totem. It is believed that the strength of the original ancestor will be passed on through the totem. A woman takes the totem of her husband upon marriage, as she is believed to now belong to his clan.

Totemism is a significant traditional practice to note because, in the context of the present study, when a child is abandoned as an infant, they oftentimes grow up not knowing which clan they belong to. This greatly impacts their sense of belonging for a length of time, way into their adulthood when they are considering cultural rites such as marriage. It is common practice that members of the same totem cannot marry, as this is considered incestuous. A child who grows up not knowing their totem could easily marry someone of the same totem without knowing, which may have deleterious effects on them. However, not much is known about this cultural practice and the impact of going against these cultural norms due to the lack of documented studies, in particular, oral histories, on the subject.

CHANGES IN SOUTHERN AFRICAN FAMILIES OVER THE LAST DECADES

History and context are both important in understanding family change. Several changes have taken place in African families since the colonisation of African states in the 1900s, where we saw new ideas of welfare being introduced. These changes are centred around the macro sociopolitical and economic shifts brought about by globalisation and modernisation that have taken place on the continent. With globalisation becoming the order of the day, individualism and liberal approaches to family life became increasingly common. Atta-Asiedu (2020) notes several changes to the African family as a result of the dual impact of globalisation and modernisation. For instance, he notes the erosion of the degree of discipline and respect that communal parenting traditionally produced due to new state policies that eventually set children against parents. The introduction of children's rights without accompanying training on their responsibilities has reportedly led to children losing respect for their parents, which is a cultural prerequisite in the African context.

Today, we see families only being able to take care of their own offspring in the nuclear setting, and families becoming smaller, which is contrary to the larger family units that included the extended family. Kinship interactions have also changed in the context of modernisation and social change. For instance, the disintegration of the extended family system was the key alternative for the welfare of OVCs. Gabrielli et al. (2018) foresaw the possibility of the extended family disintegrating when they questioned the longevity of this family form in sub-Saharan Africa.

Modernisation and the increased access to education for women as a result of feminist movements led to an increasing number of women opting to delay marriage or to remain single due to their enhanced socioeconomic status and shifting gender roles. Marriage, which was traditionally viewed as a way of organising and constituting intraethnic and interethnic social relations, has declined. Women no longer have to marry to improve their social status, and some women prefer not to deal with the patriarchal challenges of marriage in Zimbabwean society. The trends in marriage rates vary between regions: in East Asia, the rates of women entering marriage or a cohabiting union increased; in South America, the rates remained flat; and in North America and North Europe, the rates declined (Kantorová, 2013). In Southern Africa, there was a sharp decline between 2000 and 2010, from 41% to 35.3%, and for the last decade, rates of marriage have remained flat (Kantorová, 2013). As marriage has declined, cohabitation and single parenthood have increased. Advances in health care have also seen the introduction of family planning mechanisms for women to control the numbers of children they can have, which has altered household sizes significantly. In 2015, about 84.8% of women of reproductive age (15–49 years) used modern family planning methods (UN Women, 2021).

Some scholars have alluded to the resultant effects of what they view as the decline of the family using phrases including "moral decay", "cultural erosion" and "human factor decay". These scholars imply that we have digressed as a society, and this has an impact on the care and welfare of children and young people (e.g., Gwakwa, 2014; Kurevakwesu & Chizasa, 2020; Mhizha et al., 2018). These scholars attest to the fact that a combination of colonialism, globalisation, autocratic rule, corruption and recurring economic difficulties contributed to the demise of Ubuntu. Hence, alternative care models, particularly child welfare institutions, signify a decay in our moral fabric as a society.

FAMILIES IN ZIMBABWE

The study was conducted in Zimbabwe, a country in Southern Africa bordering the Republic of South Africa, Botswana, Zambia and Mozambique. Figure 5.1 shows a South African regional map indicating where Zimbabwe is located.

Families in Zimbabwe have been constructed in much the same way as most Southern African countries. In this section of the book the elements that set the Southern African family apart from families in the West are highlighted, setting up a background for the social construction of family meanings by Zimbabwean adolescents and youths in child welfare institutions.

Prominent earlier works on the African family by Marks and Rathbon (1983), Therborn (2004), Atta-Asiedu (2020) and Odimegwu et al., (2017), as well as literature reviews on the subject of family in Africa (e.g., Sooryamoorthy & Chetty, 2015), provided background information on

Fig. 5.1   Southern African regional map. Source: Kabanda, G. (2008)

families in sub-Saharan Africa. Granted, there is still a gap, especially in the literature written by African scholars on African families. There are a handful of African-based writers who have examined family as a subject of research (e.g., Allen, 2004; Therborn, 2004; Oheneba-Sakyi & Takyi, 2007). Considering the decolonisation agenda, which aims to promote scholarly research on African issues by Africans and from our perspective, this section is particularly useful in presenting an African view of family from the perspective of an African scholar. I will also allude to the dearth of family theories that are from the Global South, with most of our understanding of the concept coming from the Global North. In the absence of scholarly developments from the Global South, scholars continue to draw on Western theories to explain African families.

Table 5.1 details some key demographic features of Zimbabwe.

As the table shows, Zimbabwe is a small country with a majority of the population living in rural areas. The number of child welfare institutions

Table 5.1 Key demographic details of Zimbabwe

Indicator	Estimate	Statistics year
Total population	15,331,428	2022
Population aged 15–24	3017 (in thousands)	2020
Rural population	67.76%	2020
Number of child welfare institutions	154	2017
Population of children in institutions	Not available	
Children without parental care	26.6% of child population	2019
Life expectancy at birth	61.49 years	2019
World Bank status	Lower middle income	2020
Adult HIV/AIDS prevalence	12.9%	2022
Adolescent HIV/AIDS prevalence	12.8%	2019
Human development ranking	150 out of 189 countries	2019
Mean household composition (urban)	4.57 persons	2020
Mean household composition (rural)	5.33 persons	2020

Source: World Bank (2019, 2020, 2022)

has increased over the years, indicating an increase in the number of children in need of alternative care in the country. Unfortunately, due to a lack of proper monitoring and up-to-date records, the actual number of children in child welfare institutions in Zimbabwe is not known. Existing records indicated that there were approximately 5000 children in residential child care facilities (Chibwana & Gumbo, 2014). This number did not include unregistered facilities, which have also proliferated across the country (Southern Eye, 2013).

Families in Zimbabwe have also been impacted by socioeconomic challenges that have plunged a majority of families into poverty. Since the country gained independence from colonial rule in 1980, several policy measures were put in place to deal with the country's social and economic issues, some of which placed the country in a worse-off situation than before. One example is the Economic Structural Adjustment Program (ESAP) in the early 1990s, which saw the country implementing austerity measures that backfired on the poor majority. Social services became underfunded, and an increasing number of families could not afford to provide care for their children. The early 2000s saw an exponential increase in the number of orphans as a result of the HIV/AIDS pandemic. Many families lost individuals who left their children orphaned and in need of care. The extended family of aunts, uncles and grandparents was the intended safety net for OVCs. However, due to the rising numbers of

OVCs and worsening economic woes, the extended family could no longer cope. An increasing number of OVCs were placed in institutional care, which is supposed to be the last resort.[1] Governance issues and economic challenges have also affected Zimbabwean families. Families are straining to cater for their own in a multi-currency economy characterised by hyperinflation, rampant corruption and a lack of proper social services. The economic decline has also led to a loss of jobs as unemployment increases. More families have been forced into the informal sector, which does not offer much stability or a decent living wage. The care and welfare of children both in families and by the State child protection services under these circumstances has been compromised (Moyo & Kawewe, 2009; Mupedziswa, 2013; Mwapaura et al., 2022).

Sub-Saharan Africa is the region with the highest number of people living in poverty globally (World Population Review, 2022), and Zimbabwe is affected. Poverty remains one of the issues affecting families in Zimbabwe. UNICEF (2017) reported that 4.8 million Zimbabweans were living in poverty and 1.6 million were living in extreme poverty. In 2020, approximately 6.8 million Zimbabweans live below the food poverty line, and approximately 3.5 million children are experiencing chronic hunger (Louis, 2021). COVID-19 has exacerbated the poverty levels of most sub-Saharan African families, and Zimbabwean families are not an exception (Chingono, 2021). Currently, approximately 2.2 million children need child protection services in Zimbabwe, which will include psychosocial support and services that will address gender-based violence, violence against children and protection from sexual exploitation and abuse (UN Children's Fund, 2020). Violence and abuse of children were reported to be increasing, with 60% of reported rape survivors being mostly female children (Ministry of Public Service, Labour and Social Welfare, 2017). Families remain a salient coping mechanism in dealing with poverty and militating against societal deterioration (Moyo, 2007). Family dynamics have also changed in the last two decades, with some families reported to be experiencing relational strain, neglecting the care of children, and abusing and exploiting children. The rise in domestic violence cases in Zimbabwe has led to family dissolution and an increase in

---

[1] National Orphan Care Policy (1999)—Six-tier safety net for OVC, which included nuclear family as first option, extended family as second option, foster care with relatives as third option, community foster care as fourth option, adoption as a fifth and rarely used option, and institutional care as the last option.

female-headed households (Osirim, 2003). However, other families have remained cohesive, reciprocal, coherent and harmonious even as the effects of change threaten to destroy them (Moyo, 2007).

Zimbabwe has also seen the emergence of social orphans as a result of mass migration out of the country in search of better living conditions (Tawodzera & Themane, 2019). Social orphans have been described as children whose parents are alive but cannot provide care due to physical, emotional or economic reasons (Uasheva et al., 2014). Zimbabweans have migrated to neighbouring South Africa, Botswana, Namibia, the United Kingdom, Australia, China and several other countries. Crush et al., (2015) have described the regional migration of Zimbabweans as "temporary circular migration", which has come as a result of the crisis in Zimbabwe, and the idea is that they will return once the crisis is resolved. While the mostly middle-adult population is searching for "greener pastures", a group of young people are being *left behind* without guidance and care and are falling prey to several social ills, including drug and substance abuse, homelessness, prostitution and crime, to survive (Filippa et al., 2013; Tawodzera & Themane, 2019; Tigere & Ndlovu, 2018).

In situations of family breakdown, more young people may find themselves without adequate care and needing substitute or alternative care. Normally, young people seek refuge in the care of relatives who, in most cases, neglect or abuse them. Some young people run away from home and end up living in the streets. Once they are in the streets, government officials often round them up and place them in child welfare institutions.

DISTINCTIVE FAMILY FORMS IN ZIMBABWE

Child-Headed Families

The literature on child-headed households (CHHs) posits that they emerged as an aftermath of the HIV/AIDS epidemic in Zimbabwe. Many families lost both parents to the disease, and in the absence of extended family willing to care for the remaining orphans, families were formed that only consisted of children. Child-headed families are considered to be the most vulnerable family form, in the same category or worse than grandparent-headed families and single-parent families. They are the most vulnerable because they are, in most cases, double orphans with no living grandparents (Zagheni, 2011), so they end up caring for themselves. In particular, CHHs in rural areas and farming communities are considered the most vulnerable. In general, CHHs are vulnerable because, in this family form, children take up adult roles in the absence of their parents and adult guardians. They miss out on their childhood and opportunities to develop into fully functioning adults because of the challenges they face. Francis-Chizororo (2010, p. 712) explained it well when she stated that CHHs challenge the notion of the "ideal home, family, and normal childhood" and undermine the child rights agenda. Foster, et al., (1997) states that some CHHs are headed by children as young as 10–12 years. CHHs experience poverty that exposes them to intergenerational and transactional relationships, prostitution, substance and drug abuse, and crime, among other social issues. Due to the lack of adult caregivers in the labour market, CHHs often do not have a source of income and survive on well-wishers who know of their plight. Often, they are overlooked in society, and when they take matters into their own hands to survive, they fall prey to exploitation and abuse. Due to a lack of policy that specifically targets CHHs, they are in most cases not recipients of any social assistance. Several recommendations have been made for the government of Zimbabwe to strengthen the financial support and community structures to child-headed households so that they can meet needs related to nutrition, shelter and access to essential services.

Grandparent-Headed Families

This refers to households led by grandparents, and in Southern Africa, they are said to have also emerged as a result of the HIV/AIDS orphan crisis. Grandparents often end up caring for their orphaned or vulnerable grandchildren, even when parents are surviving and unable or unwilling to care for them (Mthembu et al., 2020; Zagheni, 2011). Due to the frailty of grandparents who, in most cases, should be recipients of care (Mhaka-Mutepfa, 2018), this family form is also considered to be vulnerable. Grandparents, similar to young children, require care and often cannot work for themselves to earn a living. This leaves them at the mercy of government assistance through pensions or social protection schemes, such as cash transfers, which in most cases in Zimbabwe are not enough to cater for these households holistically (Chikoko et al., 2021). Children in grandparent-headed families are therefore, exposed to vulnerability and poverty, which includes food and material poverty. They are also often the target beneficiaries of social protection programmes such as the Basic Education Assistance Module (BEAM), which assists them with school fees so they can access education (Ringson, 2020).

Small-House Families

The small-house phenomenon has been described as one of the factors that have led to the demise of the traditional family in Zimbabwe (Ndlovu, 2013). A "small house" is regarded as a family practice where married men maintain a single woman as a quasi-permanent sexual partner outside official marriage. The small house has also been described as an informal, long-term, secret sexual relationship with another woman who is not a man's legal wife, carried on in another residential suburb (Chingandu, 2008; Mutseta, 2016). According to Ndlovu (2013), this relationship is considered subsidiary (small) compared to the official marriage. In some cases, it becomes known by the first wife, but she will not have any power to stop it in the patriarchal context of Zimbabwe. Family scholars in Zimbabwe have found that this family setup has an impact on the socialisation and development of children as a result of absent fatherhood and lone parenthood (Muchabaiwa, 2017). It is linked to the single-parent family in that children raised in this setting often struggle with their education, identity and other development outcomes. This view might also come from the dominant heteronormative view that the nuclear family is the ideal family form for raising well-balanced children who will grow up to be fully functional adults. Scholars have debated this view with some examples of adults who were raised in single-parent homes who turned out to be fully functioning adults (see, e.g., Ford, 2017; McLanahan & Sandefur, 2009).

In summary, these three distinctive family forms included in this chapter are the ones that are most visible and that have become accepted as "normal" in Zimbabwean society. Other family forms exist, including cohabiting couples with children, single-parent families and families living apart together. This signifies a shift from the traditional family unit, which was predominantly nuclear in nature, as is the case in developed countries. However, due to the dearth of family studies in Zimbabwe, not much is known about the dynamics within these families, except for single-parent families, which have attracted some scholarly attention. What is probably more important, but missing in the Zimbabwean family literature, is information about the welfare of children and youths in these diverse family forms.

CONCLUSION

This chapter highlighted the key features of Southern African families, which is the regional context in which the study of family meanings for adolescents and youths in child welfare institutions was conducted. Families in Zimbabwe were traditionally formed along the same lines as most Southern African families, including patrilineal, matrilineal and bilateral lineages and collective communities. Of particular interest is the fact that family meanings in this region were largely still centred around kinship. The chapter also noted the changes that have taken place in Zimbabwean families, especially in light of the protracted socioeconomic and political crisis. Several key changes were highlighted, including new family forms and increasing diversity of family structures as a result of globalisation and modernisation. Some distinctive family types that can be identified in Zimbabwe are child-headed households, grandparent-led households and small-house families. These were discussed to illustrate the diversity of families in Zimbabwe compared to the rest of the region. This chapter served to acquaint the reader with the historic development of Southern African families and the current state of Zimbabwean families. In particular, the context of poverty is key because it is one of the reasons why young people end up being separated from their biological families and placed into child welfare institutions. The poverty context may also lead to strained family relations for several reasons, as families attempt to adapt to their circumstances. The example of child prostitution, increasing intergenerational relationships and out-migration of parents illustrates this point. Families are in a constant state of change, and these features may very well not be evident in the next few years; however, at the time of the study, young people were living in the social context presented here.

REFERENCES

Atta-Asiedu, K. A. (2020). *The African family in crisis: A brief analysis of the transitions and changing trends in the modern African family.* Available at SSRN 3687354.

Chibwana, M. W. T., & Gumbo, N. (2014). *Assessment report of the alternative care system for children in Zimbabwe.* (Unpublished report). Harare: SOS Children's Villages International.

Chikoko, W., Nyabeze, K., Zvokuomba, K., Mwapaura, K., & Mhizha, S. (2021). The harmonized social cash transfer program in Zimbabwe: Achievements and challenges. *Journal of Economics and Behavioral Studies, 13*(5 (J)), 12–21.

Chingandu, L. (2008). Multiple Concurrent Partnerships: The story of Zimbabwe – Are small houses a key driver? Retrieved from http://archive. kubatana.net/docs/hivaid/safaids_small_houses_070612.pdf. Accessed 7 January, 2023.

Chingono, N. (2021). Half of Zimbabweans fell into extreme poverty during COVID. Retrieved March 27, 2022, from https://www.theguardian.com/ global-development/2021/jun/21/half-of-zimbabweans-fell-into-extreme-poverty-during-covid

Crush, J., Chikanda, A., & Tawodzera, G. (2015). The third wave: mixed migration from Zimbabwe to South Africa. *Canadian Journal of African Studies/ Revue canadienne des études africaines, 49*(2), 363–382.

Filippa, O. M., Cronjé, E. M., & Ferns, I. (2013). Left behind: A qualitative study of Zimbabwean adolescents affected by parental migration. *Journal of Psychology in Society, 45,* 36–52.

Ford, D. Y. (Ed.). (2017). *Telling our stories: Culturally different adults reflect on growing up in single-parent families.* IAP.

Foster, G., Makufa, C., Drew, R., & Kralovec, E. (1997). Factors leading to the establishment of child-headed households: The case of Zimbabwe. *Health Transition Review,* 155–168.

Francis-Chizororo, M. (2010). Growing up without parents: Socialisation and gender relations in orphaned-child-headed households in rural Zimbabwe. *Journal of southern African studies, 36*(3), 711–727.

Gabrielli, G., Paterno, A., & Sacco, P. (2018). Living arrangements in sub-Saharan Africa between modernization and ethnicity. *African Population Studies, 32*(2), 4260–4272.

Gage, A. J. (1997). Women's and men's status in African families: Continuity, evolution and possible revolutions. International Union for the Scientific Study of Population (IUSSP). International Population Conference, Beijing. Liege, Belgium, 3.

Gwakwa, M. (2014). The melting pot: Where are we! The demise of the extended family system in Zimbabwe: A case of Chivhu rural communities in Chief Neshangwe area. *European Scientific Journal,* 353–364.

Kantorová, V. (2013). *National, Regional and Global Estimates and Projections of the Number of Women Aged 15 to 49 Who Are Married or in a Union,* 1970–2030. UN Population Division. Technical Paper No. 2013/2. Retrieved September 20, 2022, from https://www.un.org/en/development/desa/population/publications/pdf/technical/TP2013-2.pdf

Kurevakwesu, W., & Chizasa, S. (2020). Ubuntu and child welfare policy in Zimbabwe: A critical analysis of the national orphan care policy's six-tier system. *African Journal of Social Work, 10*(1), 89–94.

Louis, M. P. (2021). What to know about poverty in Zimbabwe. Retrieved March 21, 2022, from www.theborgenproject.org

Mafumbate, R. (2019). The undiluted African community: Values, the family, orphanage and wellness in traditional Africa. *Information and Knowledge Management, 9*(8), 7–13.

Marks, S., & Rathbone, R. (1983). The history of the family in Africa: Introduction. *The Journal of African History, 24*(2), 145–161.

McLanahan, S., & Sandefur, G. D. (2009). *Growing up with a single parent: What hurts, what helps.* Harvard University Press.

Mhaka-Mutepfa, M. (2018). Sociodemographic factors and health-related characteristics that influence the quality of life of grandparent caregivers in Zimbabwe. *Gerontology and Geriatric Medicine, 4,* 2333721418756995.

Mhizha, S., Chiroro, P., & Muromo, T. (2018). The rise in street children population in Zimbabwe as a case of human factor decay. *Review of Human Factor Studies, 24*(1), 24–45.

Ministry of Public Service, Labour and Social Welfare. (2017). National Case Management System for the Welfare and Protection of Children in Zimbabwe. Retrieved from https://www.childrenandaids.org/sites/default/files/2018-11/National%20Case%20Management%20System%20for%20the%20Welfare%20and%20Protection%20of%20Children%20in%20Zimbabwe.pdf. Accessed 7 January, 2023.

Moyo, O. N. (2007). 8-The dynamics of families, their work and provisioning strategies in the changing economies in the urban townships of Bulawayo, Zimbabwe. In *Strength beyond structure* (pp. 189–214). Brill.

Moyo, O. N., & Kawewe, S. M. (2009). Lone motherhood in Zimbabwe: the socioeconomic conditions of lone parents and their children. *Social work in public health, 24*(1–2), 161–177.

Mthembu, L. B., Poggenpoel, M., & Myburgh, C. P. (2020). Experiences of grandmothers raising their orphaned adolescent grandsons. *Africa Journal of Nursing and Midwifery, 22*(2), 17-pages.

Muchabaiwa, W. (2017). The small house phenomenon and polygyny in Zimbabwe: A problematic context for child socialisation and development. *Africology: The Journal of Pan African Studies, 10*(3), 149–162.

Mupedziswa, R. (2013). Special issue on child welfare in Zimbabwe. *Journal of Social Development in Africa, 28*(2).

Mutseta, A. (2016). The 'Small House'Phenomenon in Zimbabwe's Urban Space: Study in Glen Norah-Harare. *Open Science Journal, 1*(2).

Mwapaura, K., Chikoko, W., Nyabeze, K., Kabonga, I., & Zvokuomba, K. (2022). Provision of child protection services in Zimbabwe: review of the human rights perspective. *Cogent Social Sciences, 8*(1), 2136606.

Ndlovu, L. (2013). "Small House" Practice and its impact on the traditional family unit in Zimbabwe. In *Visions of the 21st century family: Transforming structures and identities.* Emerald Group Publishing Limited.

Oheneba-Sakyi, Y., & Takyi, B. K. (2007). *African families at the turn of the 21st century.* Greenwood Publishing Group.

Osirim, M. J. (2003). Crisis in the state and the family: Violence against women in Zimbabwe. *African Studies Quarterly, 7*(2), 154–166.

Ringson, J. (2020). Basic education assistance module as a material and psychosocial support intervention for orphans and vulnerable children in Gutu District, Zimbabwe. An evaluation. *New Ideas in Psychology, 59,* 100803.

Russell, M. (2004). *Understanding black households in southern Africa: The African kinship and western nuclear family systems.* University of Cape Town.

Sooryamoorthy, R., & Chetty, R. (2015). Studies on African families: In hindsight. *Journal of Comparative Family Studies, 46*(1), 21–37.

Southern Eye. (2013). Illegal children's homes on rise. Retrieved from https://www.newsday.co.zw/southerneye/2013/11/04/illegal-childrenshomes-rise. Accessed 7 January, 2023.

Tawodzera, M. C., & Themane, M. (2019). Schooling experiences of children left behind in Zimbabwe by emigrating parents: Implications for inclusive education. *South African Journal of Education, 39*(1), s1–s13.

Therborn, G. (2004). *African families in a global context.* (Ed) (No. 131). Nordic Africa Institute.

Tigere, R., & Ndlovu, E. (2018). Economic migration and the socio-economic impacts on the emigrant's family: A case of Ward 8, Gweru Rural district, Zimbabwe. *Jàmbá: Journal of Disaster Risk Studies, 10*(1), 1–10.

Uasheva, A., Musabayeva, A., & Rakisheva, A. (2014). Influence of personal factors to the problem of social orphanhood. *Procedia, Social and Behavioral Sciences, 143,* 288–293. https://doi.org/10.1016/j.sbspro.2014.07.407

UN Children's Fund. (2020). Humanitarian Action for Children 2021—Zimbabwe. Retrieved March 31, 2022, from https://reliefweb.int/report/zimbabwe/humanitarian-action-children-2021-zimbabwe

UNICEF. (2017). Zimbabwe: Situation of children. Retrieved April 10, 2022, from https://www.unicef.org/zimbabwe/situation-children#:~:text=Today%2C%20poverty%20has%20a%20child's,Zimbabwe%2C%2048%25%20are%20children

World Population Review. (2022). Poverty rate by country, 2022. Retrieved September 20, 2022, from https://worldpopulationreview.com/country-rankings/poverty-rate-by-country

Zagheni, E. (2011). The impact of the HIV/AIDS epidemic on kinship resources for orphans in Zimbabwe. *Population and Development Review, 37*(4), 761–783.

CHAPTER 6

Adolescents' and Youths' "Family Meanings" in Zimbabwe

This chapter details the findings from the empirical study that was conducted in child welfare institutions and with adolescents and youths in families in Harare, Zimbabwe. The research project[1] was designed to examine the social construction of the meaning of family by adolescents and youths living in selected child welfare institutions in Zimbabwe. Ribbens-McCarthy (2012) states that family meanings are not just about identifying who makes a family but also what is family. With this in mind, the study aims were twofold: (a) to examine participants' meanings of "family" by definition (family definition), asking the question *What does the term family mean to you?* and (b) to examine participants' meanings of "family" by membership (family membership, asking the question *Who is family to you?*). This chapter will cover the definitions of "family" by adolescents and youths in child welfare institutions and those of participants living in families. Participants were not asked to select responses from a preset list; therefore, no prior assumptions about their definitions of "family" were made.

---

[1] Doctoral project titled *Constructing the meaning of family in the context of biological family separation: A study of children living in institutional care and care leavers in Zimbabwe*. The project was fully funded by the Hong Kong PhD Fellowship 2016/2019.

Descriptive Statistics: Adolescents and Youths in Child Welfare Institutions

Demographic data were collected from adolescents and youths in child welfare institutions (including age, gender, schooling and reasons for admission). Table 6.1 presents the results from the descriptive statistics conducted in SPSS.

The mean age was approximately 15 years with a standard deviation of 1.760. The ages of those who completed the questionnaire were grouped into two categories: 13–17 years (adolescents) and 18–19 years (youths). The majority of the young people (90%) were aged between 13 and 17 years. As mentioned earlier, the study found that some young people who were above the age of 18 were still living in the institutions because they had not yet completed their high school education. It is against the Children's Act (Chapter 5:06) to discharge a young person if they are still pursuing their education. The youths aged over 18 in this study were reported to still be in school, and others were waiting to transition into a vocational school. The table also shows that of the study participants, the majority were in school (97%), and only 3% were not. The table also shows that there were more females than males living in institutions in this study. This finding is contrary to a previous study in Zimbabwe by Powell et al. (2004), which found more males than females in 56 institutions. The study explained how traditionally, the extended family preferred to care for girls over boys, as the former can perform cheap labour and education for the girl-child was not a priority. Unfortunately, there has been no other

Table 6.1 Demographic details of participants in child welfare institutions (%)

Descriptives	% (=435)	Standard deviation
Mean age	15.2	1.760
Mean age of admission	9.95	3.740
Male	36	
Female	64	
Schooling		
In school	97	
Not in school	3	
Precare circumstances		
Parental death	52	
Neglect	51	
Former street child	30	
Parents separated	22	
Abused	8	
Behaviour problems	5	
Previously lived with biological family	90	

national study on children in alternative care in Zimbabwe, which provides recent statistics.

A report on violence against children in Zimbabwe (University of Edinburg, Childline and UNICEF, 2016) reported that 70% of girls were victims of violence, with most girls being victims of sexual violence and boys being victims of neglect. This was a 109% increase in the number of reports of sexual abuse against girls compared to the previous reporting period. The report, however, did not indicate whether the girls ended up in alternative care for their protection. This does indicate that girls are more at risk of ending up in alternative care than boys due to their high exposure to violent circumstances. Another explanation for the higher percentage of females to males in the institutions included could be the institutional policy in some of the institutions, which ensured that boys were moved to a non-coeducational (coed) institution once they began high school (at the adolescence stage, usually 13 years). Only one of the institutions included in the sample was for boys, which may explain the lower percentage of boys in the sample.

The average age of admission into the child welfare institution was nine years. This means that the sample had fewer young people who had been separated from their birth families and entered the institution at birth. About 59% of the sample had lived in the child welfare institutions for at least five years, and 9% had lived in the institution for over ten years. The highest percentage of participants had been placed into the institution due to parental death (52%), followed by neglect (51%). A significant percentage had been rounded up from the streets by the police (30%) and placed in the institution. These young people would have run away from their birth families for several reasons, including abuse, neglect and poverty. At least 90% of the institution participants reported that they had previously lived with their birth families, which means that at least 10% had never lived with their birth families before.

The table shows that the majority of adolescents and youths in the sample had either lost a parent or were neglected by their biological family. A small percentage (8%) reported being abused prior to coming into the institution, which included both physical and sexual abuse. About 5% of the sample reported being in the institution due to behaviour problems. Usually, the higher percentages of young people with severe behaviour problems are placed in juvenile facilities, which were not included in this study. Some of the participants had experienced more than one circumstance; for instance, one could have lost a parent, then experienced neglect while living with the surviving parent or relatives or been abused. The descriptive statistics also show that the majority of young people in the sample had previously lived with their birth families (90%). This suggests that only 10% had never lived with their birth families prior to coming into the institution. These young people were either abandoned at birth or were placed in care at a very early age. This is a crucial finding for this study because it supports extant findings that show that not all young people in the institutions are orphans; they do have surviving family members who are either unwilling or unable to care for them (Williamson & Greenberg, 2010; Sherr et al., 2017).

Details of Separation Experience

Participants' length of stay in the institution helped to explain the length of time they were separated from their birth families. This was a key variable in trying to understand participants' constructions of family. Table 6.2 shows the length of stay of adolescents and youths in child welfare institutions.

The majority of the participants (59%) had lived in the institution for less than five years, and a smaller percentage (9%) of young people had prolonged stays of over ten years in the institution. On average, adolescents and youths were found to be living in institutions for slightly over five years (M=5.38, SD=3.65). The age at which young people came into the institution was also measured as a validation measure for the length of stay as well as to determine the age at which separation from the biological family occurred. As mentioned earlier, the age at which separation occurs may influence the impact of separation. The study found that participants were admitted on average during middle childhood (M=9.95, SD=3.74). The standard deviation suggests a relatively large variation in the age of admission. This implies that some young people may have been admitted at earlier ages than the average, and there are also some who are admitted later than the average.

Table 6.2 Length of stay in child welfare institution (% of participants in the sample)

Length of stay in child welfare institution	Percentage of young people
> 5 years	59
6–10 years	32
+10 years	9

Adolescents and Youths in Families
Descriptive Statistics

Participants' family demographic data were also collected and analysed descriptively as shown in Table 6.3.

The mean age of adolescents and youths living in families is also approximately 15, with a standard deviation of 1.494. Similar to the child welfare institution sample, a minority (9%) of young adults still in high school were included in the sample; however, the majority were between the ages of 13 and 17. The study found more males than females (79% males compared to 21% females) living with families. Data about the kinds of families in which adolescents lived were also collected. Participants were asked to describe their family situation. The study found a range of family types, including single-parent families (38%), extended families (24%), grandparent-headed families (12%), stepparent families (11%), and child-headed families (8%). The smallest percentage was children living with both parents (7%). It was interesting to note the low percentage of young people living in the so-called in tact families with both parents. This underscores the decline of the nuclear family ideal in Zimbabwe as well as the presence of diverse family arrangements.

Table 6.3 Demographic details of participants in families (%, means)

Descriptive statistics	Measures
Mean age	15.4 (SD: 1.494)
13–17 years	90
18–19 years	10
Male	79
Female	21
Schooling	100
Family settings	
Two-parent families	7
Single-parent families	38
Living with grandparents only	12
Living with siblings only	8
Living with extended family only (aunt, uncle, cousins)	24
Stepparent families	11

PARTICIPANT OBSERVATIONS

Observations were also used to collect data about the child welfare institutions. When the researcher visited the institutions to distribute questionnaires, they asked for a tour of each institution. The superintendents usually obliged and engaged the researcher in informal discussions that shed some light on the day-to-day life in the institution. Participant observations were carried out simultaneously with the questionnaires. Interviews were also conducted with institutional caregivers; however, these data have been published in a separate publication (Gwenzi, 2019a) and will not be presented in this book. I also spent time in the child welfare institutions and participated in some of their activities. Permission to take photographs was sought and granted by some institution managers; however, the researcher was advised not to take photographs of the children and only to photograph the surroundings and living quarters. Notes were taken to provide descriptions of the child welfare institutions, as video recording was also not allowed. The study found two main models of institutional care in operation in Zimbabwe: family-style institutions and dormitory-style institutions. Caregivers in dormitory-style institutions reported that they were in the process of making a transition to family-style institutions in line with the United Nations Guidelines for Alternative Care (United Nations General Assembly, 2010). Figure 6.1[2] shows an example of a family-style institution.

Family-style institutions were structured in such a way that one housemother lived with a minimum of eight to ten children in a cottage-style house. Usually, there was only a female caregiver, although some houses had a housemother and a housefather (a married couple) living together with the children. These caregivers had their own children at home and would live in the institution for weeks and only go to their own homes during their off-days to ensure continuity of care for young people. When they were off-duty, a stand-in caregiver would come and stay with the children. This means that there would be a change of guardians or *housemothers* based on their working shifts, but they knew they had a primary caregiver who spent the most time with them.

Family-style cottages were observed to be in a gated community, and caregivers reported during the site visits that young people living in neighbouring cottages within the same gated community would often visit each other and play in each other's yards. This kind of institution attempted to

---

[2] All the figures in this section were taken by the researcher during participant observations.

Fig. 6.1 Family-style institution in Zimbabwe

create a family environment for young people who was similar to the families in the surrounding communities. The only difference was sometimes the absence of a father figure, but in some households in the surrounding community, this is also becoming increasingly common. In contrast, dormitory-style institutions had high caregiver–youth ratios, with one caregiver having to care for 20 or more young people at a time. Attention and care will be shared among young people, usually not in equal proportions because there is only one caregiver who often works shifts. Adolescents and youths slept in gender-segregated dorms, males on their own and females on their own (see Fig. 6.2).

In the image to the left, at least ten beds are now allowed in one dormitory in an attempt to create smaller units that follow the family-style

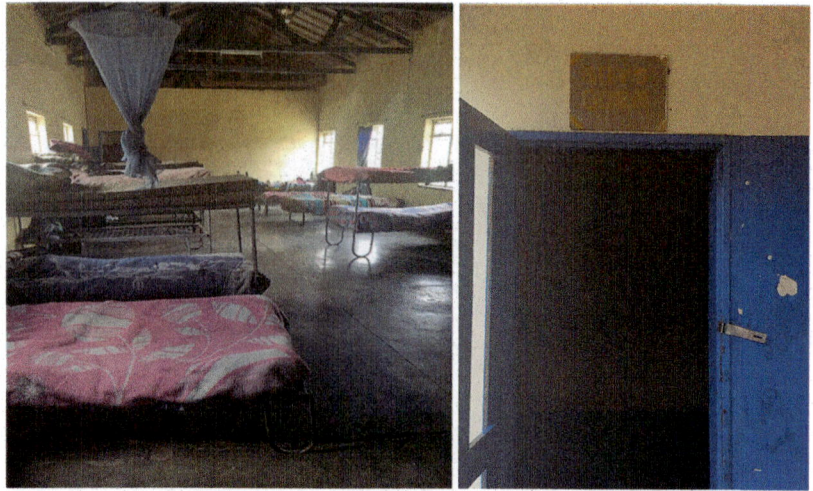

Fig. 6.2 Dormitory-style institution in Zimbabwe. (Inside a female dormitory transitioning into family style (left). Outside one of the male dormitories (right))

model. Different age groups were mixed together, which means that one could find teenagers sharing with younger children. Caregivers reported during the site observations that this increased the potential for negative peer pressure on younger children. Figure 6.3 shows an example of the structure of a dormitory-style institution that was in transition at the time of the interviews in 2017.

GROUNDED ANALYSIS ON FAMILY DEFINITIONS

Four hundred thirty-five (n=435) adolescents and youths in child welfare institutions responded to the question *what does family mean to you?* were first analysed qualitatively since they were in the form of text. The initial analysis generated categories for family definition based on the open-ended responses, thereby utilising an inductive or grounded approach. This is believed to improve the reliability of the results (Soiferman, 2010). An iterative coding process was carried out using NVivo-11 Pro software. The initial coding framework consisted of 39 definitions of "family", which were further reduced to summarised thematic categories. Table 6 presents the final thematic categories that were agreed upon by the

Fig. 6.3 Dormitory-style child welfare institution. (Outside a dormitory-style facility)

research team (researcher and study supervisors). There were four broad categories that fit young people's definitions of "family": (1) traditional definitions of family based on blood relations and kinship ties; (2) biolegal ties such as marriage, husband, wife and children (nuclear family); (3) contemporary definitions that focused on coresidence, relationships based on love and care, support and trust; and (4) definitions based on spirituality and *agape* love, which is a Christian, biblical concept of universal love. Figure 6.4 is a pie chart representation of family definitions by adolescents and youths in institutions:

Table 6.4 further details the family definitions as provided by participants in child welfare institutions.

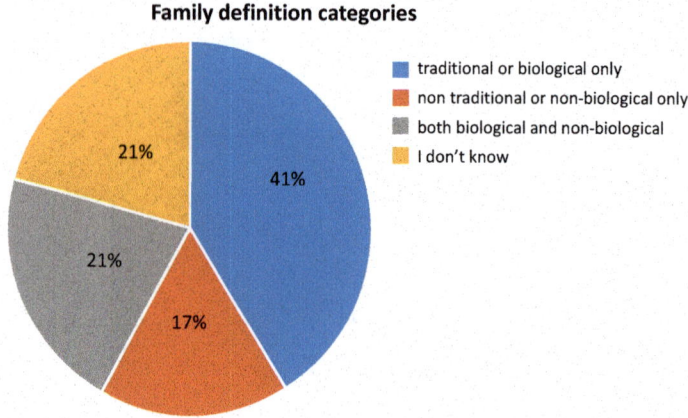

Fig. 6.4 Pie chart: family definition by participants in child welfare institutions

Table 6.4 Family definition codes

Category of family definition	Initial codes	Themes
Biological definition	• Biological family, family of origin (including extended family) • Tribe or clan membership • Children, marriage and parents • Getting married • Mother, father and children	• Blood relations • Nuclear family • Biolegal relations
Non-kin definition	• People I live with here (caregivers, housemates, institutional staff) • Friends • Foster parents • A group of people living together	• Unrelated individuals • Coresidence • Legal child welfare placements
Based on characteristics	• Based on love, care and support • Individuals who are always there for you • Bond you share • Belonging • Individuals I can trust • Togetherness and sharing things together	• Family characteristics • Family practices • Family display • Relationship quality
Other	• Family is God • God said we must love everyone	• Religion or spirituality

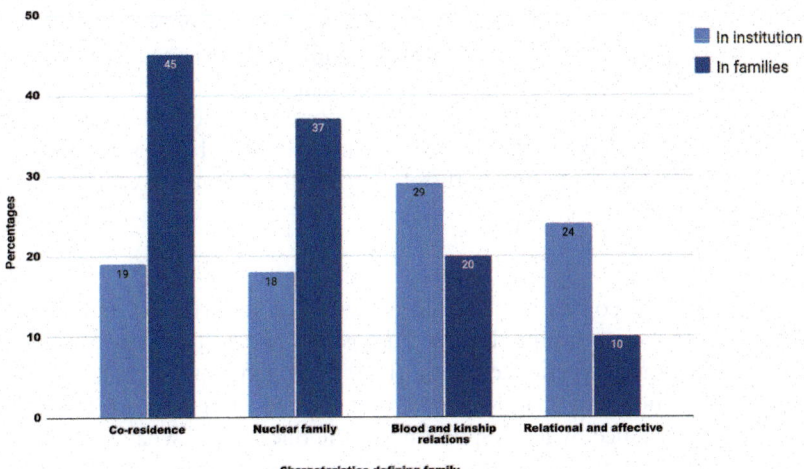

Fig. 6.5 Frequency distribution of participants' family definition categories (%)

The frequency distribution of participants' family definition categories was measured using descriptive statistics in SPSS. Figure 6.5 shows the frequency distribution by the percentage of family definition categories for both samples.

The nuclear family or biological family definition was common among the two groups of participants, with adolescents in families at 54%. Twenty-five per cent of participants in both institutions and families defined family according to support, love, care and belonging characteristics. At least 14% defined family according to both biological and non-kin characteristics. Only 2% of participants said they had no family, and 3% provided definitions that fit into the "other" category. Participants' definitions of "family" supported the contemporary definitions of "family" by sociologists (e.g., Morgan, 2011; Ribbens-McCarthy, 2012; Smart, 2011). From the analysis, the study found both biolegal and non-kin aspects being used by participants both in families and in institutions to define family. Similarly, Murray and Barnes (2010, p. 533) state that family "can be kin and non-kin, and is often about care and trust in the context of enduring relationships".

Using the text search tool in NVivo qualitative software, a further analysis was conducted to find the occurrence of words used to define family by the two groups. For example, using the word frequency function, words such as trust, continuity, belonging and protection were found to be more common in the definitions of "family" by participants in institutions than those in families. In addition, the use of the word "always" in some definitions was interpreted to mean continuity, and the text search for the word showed a higher occurrence in definitions by adolescents and youths in institutions than those in families. Some examples are noted below.

Trust
Adolescents and youths in institutions have been reported to struggle to form healthy relationships due to trust issues, the foundation of which may be negative experiences with their birth families, such as abuse, neglect, rejection and abandonment prior to their placement in the institution. For instance, when responding to the question of what a family is, one of them stated:

> *It means people whom you trust and can rely on them.* (Tamar, aged 15)

> *The people who are close to you and you trust them.* (Kundai, aged 16)

For Kundai, family also meant having a close relationship based on trust. One of the participants further stated how difficult it may be to find a trusting relationship anywhere else:

> *...family is all about trust and I don't think you can get that anywhere.* (Kuda, aged 17)

According to attachment theory, the ability to trust and relate to others is established in infancy through the quality of the infant-caregiver relationship (Bowlby, 1978). Young people whose childhoods are disrupted through separation and placed with unrelated caregivers may experience disturbances in their attachment patterns. This may explain why it was important for some institution participants to define "family" according to trust more than adolescents in families. Young people who experience separation may also experience feelings of rejection and a devalued sense of self (McDowell et al., 2019), which may affect their ability to trust others.

Continuity

The second aspect of family that was found in definitions of "family" by participants in institutions was the idea of continuity. This has been found in other studies of children in out-of-home care (Holland, et al., 2005). Continuity was interpreted from the use of the word "always" in some of the participants' family definitions. For instance, one of the participants defined family as:

> *People who help you in times of need and are **always** [emphasis added] there for you.* (Hazel, aged 17)

The word "always" is synonymous with "consistent" and "all the time", which suggests a continuing relationship. For instance, when Grace stated:

> *A family means having someone in your life who looks after you **always**.* (Grace, aged 14)

Since attachment is considered to be a part of family life (Byng-Hall, 2008), the lack of continuity affects young people's definitions of family. For adolescents and youths in institutions, the lack of continuity comes from placement instability, such as being moved from one institution to the other, which results in an increased sense of rejection and an inability to form relationships with current caregivers (Webster et al., 2000). This may also symbolise an idealised notion of "family" always being there, which makes sense considering some of the abandonment, rejection and disappointment experiences that institutionalised youths experience.

Protection

Participants also included protection in their definitions of family, which makes sense, particularly for those in child welfare institutions. When one reads the literature on young people in alternative care, their need to feel protected is a common factor (see, e.g., Christiansen et al., 2013; Wood & Selwyn, 2017; Walker, 2019). Adolescents living in families did not include this aspect in their definitions, which may imply that the idea of a family as a protective factor goes without saying. Meanwhile, for adolescents and youths in institutions, the availability of protection may not be too obvious, and stating it may be more important than those living with family. For instance, Nomusa defined family as follows:

*People who are there for me to **protect** me and take care of me.* (Nomusa, aged 16)

It was interesting to note how the protection was described in the context of a caring relationship. Similarly, the presence of love was also included, as shown in Thelma's definition below:

People who love you and protect you. (Thelma, aged 18)

For Thelma, family meant not only love but also protection, which may be critical for young people in child welfare institutions. The child welfare institution also serves as a protection mechanism by the state for vulnerable children and young people; however, the extent to which it provides this protection has been a subject of debate. The literature suggests that there have been allegations of abuse and structural neglect in the same institutions that claim to protect them (see, e.g., Juffer et al., 2017). Young people's sense of security may become even more compromised in institutional care. Their sense of security is compromised when they are in institutional care; hence, their idealised notions of "family" also contain aspects of protection.

Belonging

In terms of belonging, participants in institutions were found to emphasise a sense of belonging in their definitions, which may suggest its importance in constructing the meaning of "family". Adolescents and youths in institutions defined family as not just a group of people you are related to and/or reside with but as one of them added:

A family is a group of people where you belong. (Sibahle, aged 16)

A more detailed definition of "family" included belonging but also identity and the idea of having people you can share problems with:

You will have people with whom you will share your problems. You will feel loved and cared for. You will also have a chance to have an identity and know where you belong. Every provision will be made for you as quickly as possible. (Ruramai, aged 19)

Table 6.5 Differences between family definition aspects (in institutions vs. in families)

Aspect of family	In institutions	In families
Trust	✓	
Continuity	✓	
Belonging	✓	
Protection	✓	
Peace		✓
Without favouritism		✓

A study on care leavers in South Africa (Moodley et al., 2020) found that children in alternative care have a deep need to be cared for and belong to someone. The study also found that this need became more pertinent close to the age of leaving the institution. Care leavers try to reconnect with their roots and seek validation of their identities at this stage of emerging adulthood. This is critical because family meanings have implications that affect young people way into their adulthood.

While adolescents in families included phrases such as living in peace and in families without favouritism, these were not found in definitions by adolescents and youths in institutions. However, both groups showed that even living with the biological family is not always perfect or ideal. According to Ribbens-McCarthy (2012), the language used by individuals to describe family can contain emotions that can comprise some things that are desired and longed for, some things that are lost. Family meanings, therefore, contain a key repository of meanings and desires for togetherness and belonging, as evidenced by the views of youths in institutions. Table 6.5 illustrates the differences found in the study.

UNCATEGORISED DEFINITIONS OF FAMILY

There were some adolescents and youths who reported that they had no family (less than 1% of the total sample). Others were recorded as missing information, as they left blank responses (1%). An analysis of the demographics of the children who reported no family and the ones who left it blank showed that they were either abandoned or came into care at a very young age and that they had no knowledge of their birth families. However, it is challenging to interpret these findings because participants' negative experiences with the biological family prior may also lead to them not being willing to answer this question and leave it blank. It may also signify ambiguity in their definitions of family; either it was too sensitive or they preferred not to answer because they honestly did not know.

STATISTICAL ANALYSES OF FAMILY DEFINITIONS

After cleaning the data, dummy variables were created for each of the family definition categories above, and the responses were coded in SPSS, assigning numerical values to each category. The binary logistic regression consisted of two response categories of family definition: traditional definition (biolegal only) versus nontraditional definition (nontraditional and biolegal combined), based on the categories above. The third category consists of both the biolegal and nontraditional definitions. The fourth category, "others", was collapsed to fit into the nontraditional definition. In other words, every definition that did not fit the traditional definition of family that focused on biological and legal ties was treated as a nontraditional definition. Missing cases and "I don't know" responses were treated as missing.

Description of Variables Used in Binary Logistic Regression

Table 6.6 describes the variables in the binary logistic regression and the coding. Some of the participants experienced more than one reason for admission (e.g., had experienced parental death followed by neglect), which explains the percentages above 100% in the table.

The independent variables included participants' age, gender, living arrangement (in institution or in families), whom they go to for support and family disruption characteristics (e.g., death of a parent or parental separation) and sibling separation (whether or not young people were separated from their sibling whilst in the institution). The relationship between these variables and the family variables was tested using Pearson chi-square tests prior to running the logistic regression.

A statistically significant association was found between parental death and family definition (X^2 (df=1, n=500) < 5.783, p=0.020); however, no statistically significant association was found with parental separation (X^2 (df=1, n=500) > 0.033, p=0.856). Previous studies have also shown the importance of sibling relationships for maintaining a sense of continuity with the family for institutionalised young people and act as a buffer to the

Table 6.6 Variables in binary logistic regression and their characteristics

Description	Measures, N=534
Dependent variable	
Family definition categories (%)	
Biological or traditional	56
Nontraditional	44
Independent variables	
Age (mean)	15.2 (SD=1.634)
13–17 years	89.9%
18–19 years	10.1%
Female	56
Male	44
Child care arrangement (%)	
In institution	80
In families	20
Who do you go to for support? (%)	
Biological individuals	17
Non-kin-related individuals	70
Both biological and non-kin individuals	7
Reason for admission	
Parental death	57
Parental separation	20
Relationship perception (%)	
Poor	63
Good-excellent	37

stress related to separation (Sen & Broadhurst, 2011; Tregeagle et al., 2003). However, the Pearson chi-square test showed that sibling separation had no significant association with children's definitions of "family" (x^2 (df=1, n=500) > 1.556, p=0.212). For this reason, sibling separation was not added to the model.

Furthermore, previous literature states that the outcomes of children living in institutions largely depend on their support networks (Frimpong-Manso, 2014; Pinchover & Attar-Schwartz, 2018). Based on this evidence, support was added as a factor in the regression model because it was one of the characteristics young people used in their definitions of "family". In the literature, social support has been linked with social connectedness, social integration and identity development (Mc Mahon & Curtin, 2013). As the table shows, a large proportion of children (70%) in both institutions and families reported that they receive support from non-kin individuals. As the table shows, of the sample of young people in institutions and in families, those in institutions made up the larger portion of the sample (80%), which implies that more adolescents and youths in institutions relied on non-kin individuals than those in families. The Pearson chi-square test found a significant association between whom children go to for support and their living arrangement (χ^2 (df=2, n=500) < 74.647, p=0.00). Six per cent of the sample did not respond to the question of whom they go to for support, which was recorded as missing information. Table 6.7 shows the results of the binary logistic regression on factors influencing youth's family definitions using the Enter method. Two models were run with the first model consisting of the variables age, gender, living arrangement, parental death and parental separation, and whom they go to for support. The second model included all the variables in model 1 plus the additional variable perceptions of the relationship with the biological family.

In the first model, participants' living arrangement (whether they lived in a child welfare institution or family) and parental death were found to significantly predict their definitions of family. The results show that

Table 6.7 Binary logistic regression results with dependent variable: family definition (adjusted odds ratios and 95% confidence interval—CI)

Variables	Model 1	Model 2
Age (Ref. 13–17 years)		
18–19 years	-0.042 (0.060)	-0.039 (0.066)
In institutions	0	0
In families	1.019 (0.311) ***	0.993 (0.318) ***
Female	0	0
Male	-0.044 (0.206)	-0.065 (0.224)
Supportive individuals		
Biological	0	0
Both biolegal and traditional definition	0.158 (0.189)	-0.094 (0.293)
Type of family disruption		
Parental death (no)	0	0
Parental death (yes)	-0.723 (0.227)***	-0.608 (0.251)**
Parental separation (no)	0	0
Parental separation (yes)	-0.347 (0.272)	0.599 (0.299)
Relationship perception		
Excellent		0
Poor		0.162 (0.228)
Pseudo R²	0.058	0.059
-2 Log likelihood	504.456	503.954

adolescents living in families are more likely (odds ratio=1.019, p ≤ 0.001) than adolescents and youths in institutions to define family according to the biolegal definition than the nontraditional definition. In the second model, the variable relationship perception was added to the regression model. This speaks to the perception of youths about their relationship with the biological family. Participants' living arrangement remained constant in the second model. The results suggest that adolescents and youths in institutions are more likely than adolescents in families to define family according to the nonbiological definition.

Adolescents and youths who had lost one or both parents were found to be less likely (odds ratio=-0.723, p ≤ 0.001) than those whose parents were still alive to define family according to the biolegal definition than the nontraditional definition. This was true for both participants in institutions and in families. Similar results were found in the second model (odds ratio=0.608, p ≤ 0.001). In both models, age, gender and parental separation and who participants go to for support were not significant predictors of their choice of family definition. Participants' perceptions of their relationships with the biological family were also not significant for their family definitions.

Interpreting Binary Logistic Regression Results

Adolescents and youths in institutions are generally exposed to more non-kin individuals for their care than adolescents in families. Chapter 3 discussed the differences between familial living and institutional care, emphasising the multiple relationships to which children in institutions are exposed. The result showing that they are more likely than children in families to define family as according to the nontraditional than the traditional/biological definition is thus explained. Previous studies also emphasise the importance of institutionalised children's relationships with their social workers and caregivers (e.g., Chase, et al., 2006; Hannon et al., 2010; Winter, 2009), who are the individuals most involved in their lives. Some children in institutions have a history of negative experiences with their biological family members, which may have necessitated their need for alternative care. Previous literature supports the assertion that broken relationships with families of origin may spur the need for a broader understanding of who can be family and redefine family constellations (Lee et al., 2016).

The results also showed that children who have lost a parent are less likely than those who have not lost their parent(s) to define family according to the biological than nontraditional definition, which includes non-kin individuals. This suggests that the experience of losing one or both has an influence on family meanings. The death of a parent is reported to be one of the most stressful life events that a child or adolescent can experience (Lawrence et al., 2006). Previous studies have also found that loss disrupts and destabilises the family (e.g., Gilbert, 1996). In the event of the death of a parent, in some cases, there may be a void that can be filled by an unrelated individual in the form of a stepparent or new caregivers. For instance, if a child lost its mother, there was a higher likelihood of them being brought up by a stepmother because when a mother died leaving behind small children, the surviving husband usually remarried (Velková & Tureček, 2022). The result that adolescents and youths who have lost one or both parents are more likely to be more open to the inclusive definition of family may also be explained by the need to expand networks of care. Previous literature in sub-Saharan Africa describes how traditionally the care of orphans has always been within the biological family, including the extended family (Foster, 2000; Nyamukapa & Gregson, 2005). However, due to the pressure on the close extended family safety net, orphan care has been broadened to include distant relatives and even non-kin individuals and substitute care in institutions (Foster, 2000).

Multivariate Analysis of Adolescents' and Youths' Definitions of the Family

This section presents findings from further statistical analyses conducted on youths' definitions of family. This analysis helped to investigate the factors influencing youths' choices of family definition between the biolegal definition of family and the more inclusive definitions, which include non-kin individuals. As discussed above, the study did not find one standard definition of family for both adolescents and youths in institutions and in families. "Family" was defined according to certain characteristics that were considered to constitute "family" relationships, including blood relations, coresidence, love, support and care provision, doing things together and sharing certain experiences. These family characteristics were used to formulate categories of "family" using a grounded analytical approach, and these were the categories used in the multivariate statistical analysis. A multinomial logistic regression was performed to see the interaction of the variables with more than two categories of family definitions. First, the analysis was performed on one sample, adolescents and youths in institutions. This is because there were some independent variables that were only present for participants in institutions and not for participants in families.

The Dependent Variable

The multinomial logistic regression consisted of all the categories of family definition: traditional definition (biolegal only) versus the nontraditional definition, both the biolegal and nontraditional definition (mixed) and "others". Most participants defined family according to the biolegal definition (42%). The mixed category showed that some of the participants (21%) defined family according to both the biolegal and nontraditional definitions of family, despite the absence of the biological family in care. Missing cases and "I don't know" responses were treated as missing (code 88).

Independent Variables

Variables of interest included children's age, gender, living arrangement (dormitory or family-style institution), length of stay in the institution, family disruption or dysfunction, perceptions about the support received, knowledge of biological family and sibling separation while in the institution. Table 6.8 describes the variables used in the multinomial logistic regression analysis.

The multinomial logistic regression model was a good fit, $X^2=64.337$, ($p \leq 0.05$), pseudo $R^2=0.163$ (Nagelkerke), -2 log likelihood $= 945.899$.

Table 6.9 details the results of the multinomial logistic regression on family definition.

The results of the multinomial logistic regression reveal that for the choice between biological and nontraditional definitions of family, the results show neglect and family contact as significant variables. Adolescents and youths who reported being neglected in the biological family were approximately two times more likely than non-neglected participants to define family based on the nontraditional than biolegal definition (odds ratio = 2.083). This implies that young people who have experienced neglect prior to being placed in the institution were more open to inclusive definitions that do not only consider the biological family.

Table 6.8 Description of variables in multinomial logistic regression: participants in institutions and their characteristics

Variable	Description	Measures
Dependent variable		
Family definition		%
Biolegal or traditional		42
Nontraditional		19
Both biolegal and nontraditional		21
Others		18
Independent variables		
Mean age	Age of respondents in years (continuous variable)	15.2 (SD: 1.664)
13–17 years		90%
18–19 years		10%
Length of stay in institution	Number of years in institutions (continuous variable)	5.38 (SD 3.65)
> 5 years		60.5%
6–9 years		23.2%
+10 years		16.3%
Female		64
Male		36
Dormitory-style institution		41
Family-style institution		59
Parental death (yes)		52
Parental death (no)		48
Parental separation (yes)		20
Parental separation (no)		80
Abandoned (yes)		28
Abandoned (no)		72
Neglect (yes)		56
Neglect (no)		44
Sibling separation (yes)		20
Sibling separation (no)		
Knowledge of biological family		
I don't know my family		19
I know my family		81
Family contact (yes)		60
Family contact (no)		40
I lack support		10
I have support		90

Table 6.9 Multinomial logistic regression results with dependent variable: family definition (adjusted odds ratios and 95% confidence interval—CI)

Participants in institutions	Adjusted odds ratios (95% CI)		
Reference group=biological/traditional definition only (N=179)	Non-blood-related only (N=77)	Mixed (N=87)	Others (N=90)
Age	-0.999 (0.832–1.199)	1.069 (0.903–1.264)	-0.973 (0.816–1.160)
Length of stay	1.012 (0.927–1.105)	-0.970 (0.890–1.057)	*1.088 (0.999–1.185)
Female	1.380 (0.746–2.552)	1.148 (0.656–2.010)	1.033 (0.570–1.871)
Dormitory-style institution	-0.894 (0.481–1.659)	1.034 (0.584–1.831)	-0.949 (0.512–1.760)
Parental death	-0.948 (0.494–1.819)	1.172 (0.961–3.270)	1.584 (0.804–2.977)
Parental separation	1.880 (0.901–3.923)	1.457 (0.707–3.005)	-0.732 (0.296–1.812)
Abandonment	1.018 (0.507–2.044)	1.024 (0.517–2.028)	1.436 (0.714–2.889)
Neglect	*2.083 (1.059–4.098)	-0.829 (0.468–1.467)	-0.712 (0.383–1.324)
Sibling separation	1.167 (0.572–2.382)	-0.878 (0.435–1.773)	1.024 (0.481–2.178)
No knowledge of biological family	1.124 (0.493–2.565)	1.007 (0.452–2.245)	-0.434 (0.170–1.107)
No family contact	***2.980 (1.552–5.724)	-0.923 (0.492–1.730)	*2.183 (1.137–4.192)
I have support	-0.291 (0.108–0.783)	1.010 (0.347–2.945)	-0.626 (0.207–1.894)

Family contact was found to be significant for the choice between the biolegal definition and the nontraditional definition. The results showed that adolescents and youths who did not have contact with their birth families while in care were approximately three times more likely than children who had contact to define family according to the nontraditional definition than the biolegal definition (odds ratio = 2.980). This result implies that adolescents and youths who lacked contact may have felt a loss of "family", and when they had to consider what family means for them, they chose definitions that were based on nontraditional characteristics. Family contact was also found to be significant for the choice between the biolegal definition and "others". The "others" category has been described as including definitions such as "I have no family", "I don't know" and "God is family". The results showed that adolescents and youths who had not had contact with the biological family were approximately two times more likely than those who had contact to define family as "others" (odds ratio = 2.183). Other family characteristics, such as parental death, parental separation and separation from siblings, were not found to be significant.

The type of institution, measured as dormitory or family style, was not found to be significant for participants' definitions of family. This suggests that structural features were not as important for constructing family definitions compared to, for instance, love, care and support. The main difference between family-style institutions and dormitory ones is that the former allows for close bonds to be formed between young people and caregivers due to smaller numbers and living like a "family". However, the structure of the institution itself was not found to be significant for participants' definitions of family.

For the choice between the biolegal definition and the mixed definition (biolegal+ nontraditional), there were no significant variables in the model. For the choice between biolegal definition and "others", the length of time that adolescents and youths had been in the institution was significant. In the other choices, it was not significant. The results showed that with every one-year increase in the length of stay, young people were more likely to define family as "others". These definitions implied that young people either did not know how to define family, did not want to respond for various reasons or did not have any "family" to speak of. This was interpreted as follows: the longer the time of separation from their biological families, the more confused they may become about their family relationships, and they experience ambiguity in their definitions of family.

Participants were also asked about their perceptions of the support they received, and they had a choice of two categories, "I feel I lack support" and "I do not lack support". In the multinomial logistic regression, participants' perceptions of support were found to be a significant factor for their choice of family definition. Participants who felt they did not lack support were less likely than children who felt they lacked support to define family according to the non-kin than traditional/biolegal definition (odds ratio of 1.233). For the choice of a mixed definition and "others" categories, the support variable was not found to be significant.

Interpreting Multinomial Logistic Regression Results

The results from the multinomial logistic regression found some variables that were significantly associated with adolescents' and youths' definitions of family, namely, family contact, reasons for admission—neglect, family contact and length of stay in the institution. Few studies have explored the family definitions of children in care, but the few that have done so have had some similar findings. For instance, Sen and Broadhurst (2011) state that contact is one of the ways in which children hold on to their family origins while in care. In the absence of contact, children are unable to hold on to their birth families. Family contact has also been described as a form of family display in the context that occurs after adoption (MacDonald, 2017) and after imprisonment of a family member (Jardine, 2018).

It makes sense that the results show that children who did not have contact while in care were more likely to define family according to the nontraditional definition than the biolegal one. The nonbiological/non-traditional definition included characteristics of family display, through care, love and support. The important thing was the presence of the latter and not important who was providing such care, love and support, which opened up the possibility of non-kin individuals being considered "family". Ribbens-McCarthy (2012) stated that there is a need to recognise multiple meanings of family that are rooted in a sense of belonging and of connected selves. Where young people live, with whom and the interactions they experience all contribute to their sense of belonging. Contact also signifies the continuity of relationships, which is one of the aspects that adolescents and youths described in their definitions of family. Continuity has long been linked with belonging for children in care (Hillan, 2008; Holland, 2010; Naert et al., 2017). Family relationships provide a significant source of continuity of care throughout a child's lifetime.

Young people's precare circumstances have also been described as having important influences on their relationships, including with family. Young people with a history of negative experiences in their biological family, such as neglect, abandonment and abuse leading to them being removed and taken into substitute care, have their relationship affected. The study found neglect to be significant for participants' definitions of family, with those who had been neglected being more open to the non-biological definition of family than the biological definition. This showed an openness to include non-kin individuals or characteristics that were not based on consanguinity after experiencing neglect by the biological family. Studies about fictive kin support this argument. Fictive kin, who are not based on blood relations or legal ties, become necessary when a deficit is found in the biological family (Braithwaite et al., 2010). Some studies have also described fictive kin as an informal support system (e.g., Shklarski et al., 2015).

Adolescents and Youths' Family-Related Worries

The mental health of young people in institutions has been well studied, and one of the mental health problems found among them was excessive worry (see, e.g., Denton et al., 2017; Moreno-Manso et al., 2018). Similarly, youths with a history of institutionalisation have been reported to have elevated levels of anxiety, among other mental health issues (Bos et al., 2011). Previous studies have also found that young people in alternative care are concerned about their birth families and often spend much time worrying about them (Sen & Broadhurst, 2011). With this background, the next part of the qualitative analysis explored adolescents' and youths' worries. Both participant groups (in families and in institutions) were asked questions related to the frequency of their worries and what they worried about the most. Figure 6.6 details the frequency of worry

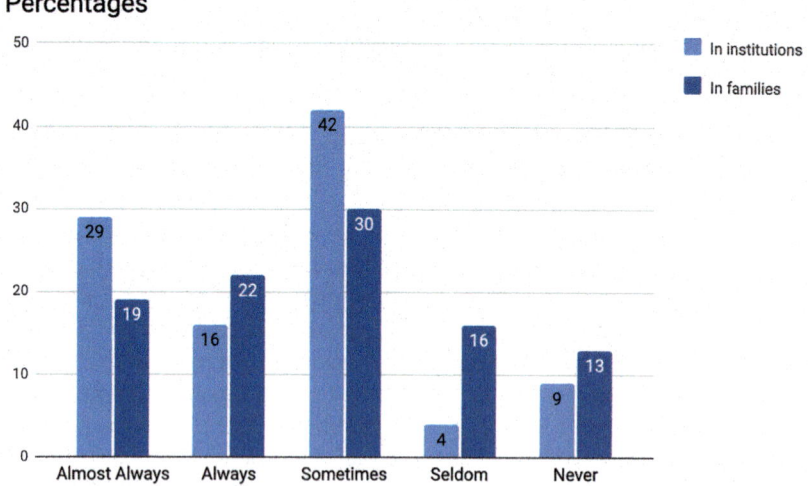

Fig. 6.6 Frequency distribution of participants' worrying patterns (%)

among children in institutions and children in families based on Likert scale responses from almost always worried (5) to never worried (1).

The graph shows that on average, for those involved in the study, those in institutions reported worrying more often (ranging from almost always to sometimes) than participants in families. The frequency of worrying was higher for most of the response categories for participants in institutions (e.g., 29% of participants almost always worried compared to 19% in families). When asked what they worried about, adolescents and youths reported more worries related to the biological family, even during separation. Just because they were separated from their biological family did not mean that they stopped worrying about them. Some institution participants worried about not seeing members of their biological family for several years and often wished they could do so.

Adolescents in families reported more worries related to their physical needs being met, for instance, not having money for food and school fees. Despite living with their birth families, the context of poverty in Zimbabwe exposed young people to deprivation and food poverty (Chingono, 2021). In contrast, adolescents and youths in institutions often meet their physical needs in child welfare institutions. This is often the priority, while emotional needs are not adequately met. Adolescents and youths in institutions were more worried about how their physical needs would be met, leaving the child welfare institution as adults.

An analysis that included a text search for family-related themes among the participants' responses provided a few examples. These are detailed in Table 6.10.

The table shows that even during separation, participants thought about and worried about their biological family members. Others who did not have a biological family to speak of as with Lucie worried whether she

Table 6.10 Examples of participants' family-related worries

What do you worry about?	Growing up without a family (Thando, 15)
	Finding a family who loves me (Lucie, 14)
	My mother is sick and I can't live with her (Melody, 13)
	I worry because my mother has no money and she cannot take care of me (Gamuchirai, 15)
	Where would I go when I am not wanted at the institution and who do I trust for my help and who can stand by my side as I was rebuked by my own family long time ago and who would be responsible for the needs I require for life as other children in society (Tafadzwa, 17)

would find a family that would love her. She was possibly considering the possibility of being placed in foster care. Thando worried about growing up without a family because, for her, it appears she had not found a "family" in the child welfare institution. Tafadzwa worried about where he would go after leaving the institution because he recognised the importance of family as a source of help and support, and from his response, his own family was not an option.

As evidenced by the analysis of what participants worried about, 31% of institutionalised youths' worries were related to the biological family. Participants continued to think and worry about their birth families even during separation. This is where the notion of ambiguous loss was found to be applicable. The biological family remained "physically absent, but psychologically present" (Boss, 2006). Holland and Crowley (2013, p. 61) described this phenomenon as "the emotional copresence of the birth family" and noted how children living in substitute care carried on into adolescence and adulthood. This has also been confirmed by a longitudinal study that followed care-experienced youths as adults (e.g., Fargas-Malet & McSherry, 2021). Munro (2001 as cited in Atwool, 2013, p. 183) noted how "birth mothers, in particular, remained vivid and central characters in their lives regardless of the child's length of time in care, the reasons they gave for their admission to care, or their satisfaction with their placement". McWey and Cui (2021) found that with more regular contact with the biological family while in care, there are fewer mental health symptoms among youths in the child welfare system. The pervasive nature of the blood relationship was also evidenced in participants' definitions of family, which were predominantly of the traditional or biolegal category. This has also been noted in previous studies in both Western cultures and in the Global South (e.g., Cheney, 2016; Logan, 2013).

Broader Family Definitions Beyond Blood Relations

What does all this mean? The findings suggest that adolescents' and youths' definitions of family are broad; they not only are based on blood or biolegal ties but also consider unrelated individuals and characteristics that go beyond consanguinity. Certain practices, such as support, love and care, were found to be important in defining family, in line with contemporary literature on the meaning of family. A deeper exploration of participants' open-ended responses, which led to the final categories of family definition described in the previous section, revealed some subtle but nuanced characteristics pointing to what young people require most from "family" for them to define it as such. For instance, the use of certain words highlighted the need for belonging, continuity, trust and protection from those who are regarded as family.

The study results support the growing literature on the importance of the distinction between biological and social kinship, biological and social parenting, and the biological and social construction of the family (Logan, 2013). There are many implications that can be drawn from these findings. As a starting point, any policy or practical interventions aimed at improving the lives of young people in child welfare institutions may benefit from a consideration of broader family definitions. This requires an overall acknowledgement of the different family configurations that young people in nonnormative arrangements identify with based on the circumstances surrounding their lives. This is similar to the analysis by Widmer (2016) on the need to take into account more relationships as "family". He called this the "configurational perspective" on families, which traces complex patterns of emotional, cognitive and practical interdependencies among large numbers of family members beyond the nuclear family (p. 8).

Most young people in child welfare institutions are separated from their biological families because of some dysfunction in their birth families. Globally, millions of children live in institutions. This group of children and youths is not a homogeneous group; some have lost one or both parents, while others ("social orphans") have both parents who are unwilling or unable to provide care. These circumstances affect how young people make sense of their family relationships at any given point. We cannot use taken-for-granted notions of family as a blanket for all young people without considering those who live in different contexts. This approach recognises the diverse living contexts and day-to-day realities of the lives of young people, which is more holistic and youth focused.

Furthermore, the sociology of family helps to explain the importance of non-kin bonds, which, in this study, were equally important for adolescents and youths as much as blood relations. The implication of this is that practitioners should encourage and nurture not only blood-related relationships but also non-kin relationships with individuals with whom young people grow attached to and recognise as potential families. The focus on blood relationships alone limits the nature of relationships that are possible for young people in child welfare institutions, especially after considering their previous circumstances. Widening the network of people who could be described as family will benefit young people whose blood relationships are either strained or not available.

ADOLESCENTS' AND YOUTHS' FAMILY MEMBERSHIP IN ZIMBABWE

The previous subchapter focused on adolescents' and youths' constructions of family by definition. In this chapter, the focus is now on constructions of family by membership. The findings in this part focus on participants' responses to the question, *who is family to you?* Family membership is usually "conferred on children by their parents and other relatives from the moment of birth and it is a vital strand of healthy emotional and psychosocial development" (Schofield & Beek, 2005, p. 19). However, for adolescents and youths in institutions, the context of separation from the biological family might complicate constructions of their *family membership*. Similar to the family definition analysis described in the previous part, an initial thematic analysis of the open-ended responses in the questionnaire was conducted to determine the categories of family membership. Table 6.11 shows the four categories of family membership that came from the analysis.

Similar to the analysis on family definition, an initial qualitative analysis of the open-ended responses in the questionnaire was conducted to determine the categories in the dependent variable. Figure 6.7 shows the frequency distribution (in percentages) of the categories of who counts as "family" among youths in institutions and youths in families, in this case referring to individuals and not characteristics as in the family definition.

The graph shows that compared to youths in institutions, youths in families consider biological individuals to be "family" more than non-kin individuals. Very few of the adolescents in families included non-kin

Table 6.11 Categories of family membership in institutions

Family membership categories	Percentage (N=435)
Biological family members (e.g., mother, father, siblings)	46
Nonbiological members (e.g., caregivers, foster parents)	29
Both biological and non-kin individuals (e.g., biological mother, foster mother)	12
Others (e.g., God, no family)	13

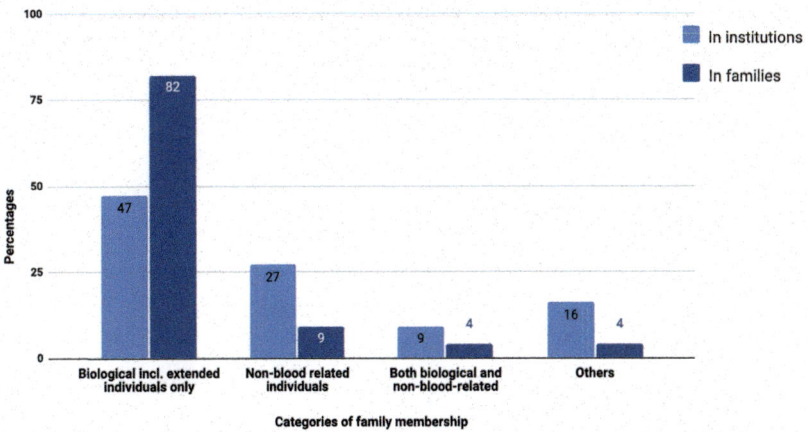

Fig. 6.7 Frequency distribution of family membership (%)

individuals as "family", with percentages less than 10%. Twenty-seven per cent of participants in institutions listed non-kin individuals as "family". The latter findings are similar to the analysis on family definitions, which showed that compared to institutionalised participants, adolescents in families are not as exposed to non-kin individuals as caregivers. In other words, adolescents and youths in institutions are more likely to view non-kin individuals as "family" than adolescents in families. Adolescents and youths in institutions also tended to include both biological and non-kin individuals as family more than children in families (9% compared to 4%), although both percentages were lower than biological and non-kin individuals only. This may be explained by the increased exposure of young people in institutions to non-kin individuals in their daily lives, as explained in Chap. 4.

Statistical Analysis of Adolescents' and Youths' Constructions of Family Membership (in Institutions and in Families)

The dependent variable had four categories describing who was considered "family": biological only, non-kin individuals only, both biological and non-kin individuals (mixed category), and others. Because of the number of categories, a multinomial logistic regression analysis was found to be appropriate. Both participants in families and in institutions were

Table 6.12   Description of variables in regression analysis on family membership: in institutions and in families

Variables	Description	Measures
Dependent variable		
Biological only		47
Non-kin only		28
Both biological and non-kin		9
Others		16
Age	Age in years (continuous variable)	15.2 (SD: 1.634)
13–17 years		89.9%
18–19 years		10.1%
Female		56
Male		44
Child care arrangement (%)	Where participants lived	
In institution		80
In families		20
Who do you go to for support?		
Biological individuals		20
Both biological and non-kin		81
Reason for admission		
Parental death	Yes	58
Parent(s) still alive		42
Parents separated		19
Parents not separated		81
Relationship perception		
Poor		63
Good-excellent		37

included in the analysis. Table 6.12 describes the variables in the analysis, which were comparable between both youth groups.

Pearson chi-square tests were conducted to determine which variables were significantly associated with constructions of their family membership. The results found that there was a significant association between participants' living arrangement (whether they lived in a child welfare institution or with their birth families) and their construction of who counts as "family" for them (X^2, df = 2, n=534, p ≤ 0.01). A significant association was also found between participants' ages and family membership (X^2, df = 12, n=534, p=0.01). Some family experiences were also tested using the Pearson chi-square test. Parental death and parental separation were the two common experiences between the two groups of young people. Neither experience was found to be significantly associated with constructions of their family membership. Support was found to be significantly associated with family membership (X^2, df = 4, n=534, p ≤ 0.01). Participants reported three categories of individuals they go to for support: biological (blood-related) individuals, non-kin individuals and both biological and non-kin individuals combined. Last, participants' perceptions of their relationship with their biological family members were also measured using chi-square tests to see if they were significantly associated with family membership. The test found that children's perception (measured as poor or good; from the Likert scale response from excellent=5 to poor=1) was significantly associated with constructions of who counts as family (X^2. df=2, n=534, p=0.02). The results of the multinomial logistic regression are shown in Table 6.13.

Table 6.14 details the results of the second model, which measured biological only versus mixed family composition.

In the first model, the table shows that with every one-year increase in age, youths were less likely to include biological individuals as family than non-kin individuals (odds ratio=-0.799). In the second model, the results also show that with an increase in age, youths were less likely (odds ratio= -0.862) to include biological individuals only as family than both biological and non-kin individuals combined. This is in line with previous findings by Morrow (1998), who found that older children are

Table 6.13 Model 1 results of multinomial logistic regression when dependent variables are family membership categories (adjusted odds ratios and 95% CI)

	Odds ratio (95% CI)	Odds ratio (95% CI)
Variables	Biological only vs. non-kin only	Mixed vs. non-kin only
Age	**-0.799 (0.68–0.93)	-0.927 (0.74–1.16)
Female	**-0.483 (0.28–0.82)	*-0.454 (0.21–1.16)
Child care arrangement		
In families	***5.810 (2.50–13.51)	-0.940 (0.24–3.68)
Who do you go to for support?		
Biological individuals	1.159 (0.49–2.76)	-0.552 (0.18–1.72)
Non-kin individuals	1.628 (0.56–4.69)	1.901 (0.50–7.23)
Reasons for admission		
Parental death	1.463 (0.84–2.57)	1.588 (0.68–3.70)
Parental separation	*2.147 (1.06–4.34)	2.324 (0.85–6.36)
Poor perception	*-0.589 (0.35–0.99)	-0.856 (0.39–1.88)

Reference category: non-kin individuals only

Table 6.14 Model 2 results of multinomial logistic regression when dependent variables are family membership categories (adjusted odds ratios and 95% confidence intervals)

	Odds ratio (95% CI)
Model variables	Biological only vs. mixed
Age	**-0.862 (0.70–1.06)
Female	1.064 (0.51–2.27)
Child care arrangement	
In families	***6.183 (1.87–20.44)
Who do you go to for support?	
Biological individuals	2.100 (0.72–6.13)
Non-kin individuals	-0.856 (0.26–2.83)
Family disruption characteristics	
Parental death	-0.922 (0.42–2.05)
Parental separation	-0.924 (0.37–2.29)
Poor perception	-0.688 (0.33–1.45)

Reference category: both biological and non-kin individuals

less likely to view family as formal, blood relationships; rather, they focus more on relationship quality than younger children. According to Morrow (1998), this signifies a developmental sequence in the acceptance of different family situations and that it reflects a more sophisticated cognitive reasoning in older children as they construct who is family for them.

In the first model, females, compared to males in both institutions and families, are less likely to include biological individuals only as family than non-kin individuals (odds ratio = -0.483). Females are also less likely to include both biological and non-kin individuals (odds ratio= -0.454) than non-kin only. This is contrary to previous findings that found no association between gender and children's family concept (Morrow, 1998). Previous studies have found that females have a stronger attachment to their biological parents than males, continuing to rely on them for support even in adolescence, while males are more likely to decrease their reliance while preferring peer support (Paterson et al. 1994). Unfortunately, no recent findings exist (to the author's knowledge) on the relationship between gender and the construction of family membership. The second model did not show significant results for gender.

Participants' living arrangements (whether in families or in child welfare institutions) were also significant in both models. The results show that adolescents in families are approximately five times more likely to include biological individuals as family than non-kin individuals (odds ratio= 5.810). The results for the mixed and non-kin categories were not significant. In the second model, participants in families were more likely (odds ratio= 6.183) than participants in institutions to include biological individuals than both biological and non-kin individuals combined. This finding supports the analysis of family definitions described in the first section of this chapter, where participants in families were also found to be more likely to define family according to biological or biolegal definitions compared to adolescents and youths in child welfare institutions. The same explanation applies here: participants in institutions may be more exposed to non-kin individuals for their care than participants in families. The need for non-kin caregivers or fictive kin usually comes during special circumstances when the biological family, including extended family, is unable or unwilling to provide care. The concept of fictive kin suggests that when there is a deficit in the biological family, fictive kin networks are usually formed to replace or perform the functions that the biological family cannot (Braithwaite et al., 2010).

Parental separation was found to be a significant factor in participants' constructions of their family membership. The study found that adolescents and youths whose parents have not separated were more likely (odds ratio= 2.147) than those whose parents separated to include only biological individuals than non-kin individuals. Many studies have examined children whose parents have separated and the effect that disruption has on their family lives. Some of these studies have found that when parents separate, one parent removes of the family home and becomes an absent parent. Some of the parents remarry, bringing new unrelated partners in the home (e.g., Pryor & Rogers, 2001; Ganong et al., 1999; Seltzer & Brandreth, 1994). Pauline and Boss (2009) describe the ambiguous loss that children experience when their parents separate. This may explain the need to open up a more inclusive definition of family that includes non-kin individuals. The second model did not show any significant results for parental separation and family membership.

Participants' perceptions of their relationship with their biological family members were found to be significant in the choice between biological individuals and family non-kin individuals. Participants with poor perception of their relationship with the biological family were found to be less likely than those with excellent relationship perception (odds ratio = -0.589) to include biological individuals as family than non-kin individuals. Having a family sense of belonging has been associated with perceptions about relationship quality (e.g., King et al., 2015). The second model did not show any significant results for participants' relationship perceptions and family membership.

Adolescents' and Youths' Constructions of Family Membership (in Institutions Only)

The abovementioned section focused on a combined sample of adolescents in families and those in child welfare institutions. The results from the multinomial logistic regression above showed that participants' living arrangements, their age and gender and their perception of their relationship with the biological family influenced whom they counted as "family". The next analysis is focused only on the sample of adolescents and youths in child welfare institutions. This is because there were some variables that applied to participants in institutions that did not apply to participants in families, and these were mostly related to the child welfare institution environment (e.g., the presence of family contact and support), precare circumstances and length of time separated from the biological family. The dependent variable consists of three categories of family membership: biological individuals only, non-kin individuals only and both biological and non-kin individuals combined. Table 6.15 describes the variables that were added to the model for adolescents and youths in institutions.

The results from the multinomial logistic regression are presented in Table 6.16:

Interpreting Family Membership Results

The regression analysis revealed that for the choice of who counts as family, some variables that were not significant for family definitions are now seen as significantly associated with family membership constructs. The results show that age is a significant factor in who participants included as family. Older youths aged 18–19 were more likely than younger adolescents aged 13–17 to include non-kin individuals as family than non-kin individuals only (odds ratio= 0.166). This suggests that with an increase in age, young people in institutions are more open to inclusive family compositions, which include non-kin individuals. These findings are similar to those of a previous study by Morrow (1998), who found that older children are less likely to view family as formal, blood relationships but focus

Table 6.15 Description of variables in multinomial logistic regression: family membership in child welfare institutions (%, means)

Variables	Measures
Age	M=15. 2 S.D 1.664
13–17 years	90%
18–19 years	10%
Length of stay	M=5.38 years S.D 3.651
> 5 years	60.5%
6–10 years	23.2%
+10 years	16.3%
Female	64
Male	36
Dormitory-style institution	43
Family-based style	57
Separated from sibling (s)	*18*
Not Separated from sibling (s)	82
Parent(s) death (Yes)	55
Parent(s) death (No)	45
Parents not separated	78
Parents separated	22
Experienced abuse	9
Did not experience abuse	91
Experienced abandonment	*25*
Did not experience abandonment	76
Experienced neglect	*61*
Did not experience neglect	39
Had family contact	*75*
No family contact	25
Who do you go to for support	
Non-kin individuals	78
Biological individuals	12
Both biological and non-kin	9
Excellent relationship with birth family	58
Poor relationship with birth family	42

more on relationship quality than younger children. According to Brannen and O'Brien (1996) and Morrow (1998), this signifies a developmental sequence in the acceptance of different family situations and that it reflects a more sophisticated cognitive reasoning in older children as they construct who is "family". Variables such as length of stay in the institution, type of institution and some reasons for admission, such as parental death, parental separation and neglect, were not found to be significant for family membership constructions.

Table 6.16   The results of the multinomial logistic regression on family membership in institutions (adjusted odds ratios and 95% confidence intervals)

Adjusted odds ratios (95% CI)

Reference group=biological individuals only (N=151)	*Non-kin only (N=95)*	*Biological and non-kin combined (N=75)*
Age (ref: 18–19 years)		
13–17 years	***0.166 (0.060–0.460)	0.608 (0.182–2.025)
Length of stay (ref: +10 years)		
> 5 years	0.304 (0.099–0.930)	0.579 (0.165–2.025)
6–10 years	0.336 (0.108–1.045)	0.556 (0.154–2.008)
Gender (ref: female)		
Male	0.418 (0.227–0.769)	0.675 (0.363–1258)
Type of institution (ref: family style)		
Dormitory-style institution	1.233 (0.675–2.252)	1.350 (0.736–2.477)
Parent(s) death as reason for admission (ref: yes)		
Parent(s) death (no)	1.088 (0.557–2.126)	0.618 (0.308–1.242)
Parental separation as reason for admission (ref: yes)		
Parental separation (no)	1.304 (0.585–2.910)	1.198 (0.531–2.703)
Abandonment as reason for admission (ref: yes)		
Abandonment (no)	***0.274 (0.132–0.568)	0.260 (0.123–0.548)
Neglect as reason for admission (ref: yes)		
Neglect (no)	1.165 (0.624–2.177)	1.1.65 (0.623–2.178)
Sibling separation (ref: yes)		
Sibling separation (no)	1.707 (0.757–3.848)	1.340 (0.611–2.937)
Family contact (ref: yes)		
Family contact (no)	1.874 (0.917–3.830)	1.048 (0.497–2.211)

(*continued*)

Table 6.16 (continued)

Adjusted odds ratios (95% CI)		
Reference group=biological individuals only (N=151)	*Non-kin only (N=95)*	*Biological and non-kin combined (N=75)*
Who do you go to for support? (ref: no support)		
Support from non-kin	0.694	***0.041 (0.004–0.374)
Support from biological individuals	(0.037–12.896) 0.630	*0.048 (0.005–0.488) **0.037 (0.003–0.422)
Support from both biological and non-kin	(0.030–13.038) 0.562	
	(0.025–12.455)	
Relationship perception (ref: excellent)		
Poor relationship perception	1.158	1.735 (0.591–5.098)
	(0394–3.409)	

Ref: biological individuals only

Abandonment as a reason for admission was found to be significant for the choice between biological individuals as family and non-kin individuals as family. The results show that participants who did not report abandonment as their reason for being in the child welfare institution prior were more likely to include biological individuals as family than non-kin individuals (odds ratio=0.274). In other words, participants who reported abandonment were more likely to include non-kin individuals as "family". Previous studies have found that abandoned and orphaned children who are brought up in institutions suffer from a range of social, psychological and economic problems (Gilborn et al., 2006; Zhou, 2012). Some of the psychological issues are related to the loss they experience when they are separated from the biological family. Abandoned children, in particular, may experience attachment disorders, which may include indiscriminate behaviour, and placement in families improves children's attachment status (Smyke et al., 2010). In the absence of biological family members, non-kin individuals are considered family members.

Gender results were not significant for constructions of family membership. Participants' perceptions of their relationship with their biological

families were not found to be significant for family membership constructions. Where participants go to for support was found to be significant for
who they included as "family". The results show that those who receive
support from non-kin individuals only are more likely to include both
biological and non-kin individuals as family than biological only (odds
ratio =0.041). In addition, participants who received support from biological individuals only were also more likely to include both biological
and non-kin individuals as family than biological only (odds ratio=0.048).
Furthermore, youths who received support from both biological and non-
kin individuals were more likely to include both biological and non-kin
individuals as family than biological only (odds ratio=0.037). Families of
choice represent a postmodern view of family sociology that places emphasis on the creation of networks of relationships that are conceived based on
the provision of support, care and commitment (Weeks et al., 2001).
Hence, support is a crucial factor in the construction of family membership, as supported by the findings in the present study. The availability of
individuals in one's social network also contributes to their inclusion as
family members, provided there is frequency of contact and good quality
of relationships (Davies, 2012; Stoilova et al., 2017). Becker and Charles
(2006) describe the provision of support as an example of "doing family",
which supports Morgan's (2011) *family practices* concept.

Broader Family Membership Categories

The analysis helped to identify some of the factors involved in constructing the family lives of adolescents and youths in child welfare institutions,
showing how the blood relationship is not all that matters when considering who is family and who is not. Finch (2007, p. 69) stated that understanding the meaning of family is not only about who belongs and who
does not, but it involves certain "practices, identities and relationships".
The study found three categories of who is considered "family", including
individuals who fit into the biolegal category, non-kin individuals and a
mixed group of both biolegal and non-kin individuals. However, certain
factors were also considered that influenced the inclusion and exclusion of
certain individuals from these groups.

The results show that there are multiple factors that influence young
people's constructions of their family membership. Participants' precare
circumstances are contributing factors, in this case, abandonment, which
was found to be significant for all the configurations of family

membership. Individual factors, such as age, were also contributing, and differences were found between older youths and younger youths. This is similar to previous studies (e.g., Morrow, 1998), which show a developmental sequence in the understanding of family.

Another subjective factor that was found to be significant was participants' perceptions of their relationship with the biological family. As previously described, where participants perceived their relationships as poor, they were less likely to consider those individuals as family, and this was related to the quality of the relationship, more than family structure or blood relationship. King and Boyd (2016) state that the perception of family belonging, which encompasses feelings of inclusion in one's family, is influenced by the quality of the relationship. Institutional factors such as length of stay and the type of institution also contributed to participants' constructions of their family membership. Prolonged stays in the institution were found to weaken the ties between the young people and their birth families, leading to a reduced likelihood of family reunification and increased behavioural issues, which is in line with previous findings (e.g., Frimpong-Manso & Bugyei, 2019; López & del Valle, 2015).

In Zimbabwe, traditionally, the extended family would step in during instances when the birth family failed or became incapacitated to play their parenting role for several reasons, including illness, death or poverty (Masuka et al., 2012; Chinyenze, 2017). However, the capacity of the extended family to care for OVCs has been attenuated, as explained in previous chapters, and therefore, non-kin individuals can be a useful resource for the care of young people without adequate care. For the adolescents and youths in the Zimbabwe study, in the absence of the birth family, fictive kinship relationships were formed with caregivers and other unrelated individuals who provided support. A study by Gayapersad et al. (2019) in Kenya found that young people were able to find "family" in a child welfare institution, particularly family-style institutions. Similar to the Zimbabwe study, orphans and separated children in the Kenya study redefined the traditional concept of family based on consanguinity to one composed of non-kin providing care and support. The process of deciding who counts as family, therefore, could be described as a process of seeking out alternative sources for the provision of care and support.

Several implications can be drawn from these findings, including the need to rethink what family means for adolescents and youths in child welfare institutions. The study has shown that family members are no longer just blood-related individuals but also non-kin individuals. In the absence of the birth family, alternative sources of support from friends, community members and significant others can be a valuable resource that has been considered more in the line of foster care and community care but not as "family". This may be because our culture still sticks to heteronormative understandings of what a family is. However, this may need to be reconsidered when we are thinking about young people who live in contexts of separation from the birth family for periods of time, some for their whole childhood. The discussions about who is family for young people in institutions need to begin years before they are expected to exit the institution. This will allow them to reflect on and think about the individuals who are significant in their lives, and they need to understand that the definitions need not be narrow or focused on just their blood relations because these are often not available or willing to provide care.

CONCLUSION

This chapter detailed the findings from the study on adolescents' and youths' constructions of family by definition and membership. The mixed-method study necessitated mixed analyses, including descriptive statistics, thematic analysis of qualitative data and some statistical analyses, namely, chi-square tests and logistic regressions. The results showed that there is no definition of family by young people in Zimbabwe's child welfare institutions. Adolescents and youths defined family according to biological/traditional definition, non-kin definition which included certain characteristics, such as love, care and support as determinants of the family relationship, and a combination of both the biological and non-kin definition, which included both biolegal and affective characteristics. A fourth category of "others" included definitions such as "I don't have a family" or family is everyone, which signified ambiguity in constructing the meaning of family for some participants in child welfare institutions. Some factors were found to be significant for constructions of family by definition, namely, family contact while in the child welfare institution, neglect prior to placement in the institution and length of stay in the institution. Some of the results were compared to a sample of participants in families, and a few differences were found.

Similar to the analysis on family definition, a combination of analyses, including descriptive statistics, thematic analysis of qualitative data and some statistical analyses, namely, chi-square tests and logistic regressions, were carried out for the family membership dependent variable. The results showed that participants constructed categories of family member-ship based on biological individuals only, non-kin individuals only and a combination of both biological and non-kin individuals. Some factors were found to be significant for young people's constructions of family membership, namely, age, abandonment prior to placement in the institu-tion and support from biological individuals and non-kin individuals. Some of the results were compared to a sample of young people in fami-lies, and the study found age and living in families to be significant factors. The experience of living with one's biological family exposed young peo-ple to less non-kin individuals compared to living in a child welfare institu-tion. Adolescents and youths in families were therefore more likely than the sample in institutions to include biological individuals as family than non-kin individuals. Older youths in both families and institutions were also more open than younger youths to broader family configurations, which included non-kin individuals.

REFERENCES

Atwool, N. (2013). Birth family contact for children in care: How much? How often? Who with? *Child Care in Practice, 19*(2), 181–198.

Becker, B., & Charles, N. (2006). Layered meanings: The construction of 'the family' in the interview. *Community, Work and Family, 9*(2), 101–122.

Boss, P. (2006). *Loss, trauma, and resilience: Therapeutic work with ambiguous loss.* WW Norton & Company. New York.

Bos, K., Zeanah, C. H., Fox, N. A., Drury, S. S., McLaughlin, K. A., & Nelson, C. A. (2011). Psychiatric outcomes in young children with a history of institu-tionalization. *Harvard Review of Psychiatry, 19*(1), 15–24.

Bowlby, J. (1978). *Attachment.* Retrieved March 18, 2017, from https://psycnet.apa.org/record/1982-00026-001

Braithwaite, D. O., Bach, B. W., Baxter, L. A., DiVerniero, R., Hammonds, J. R., Hosek, A. M., et al. (2010). Constructing family: A typology of voluntary kin. *Journal of Social and Personal Relationships, 27*(3), 388–407.

Brannen, J., & O'Brien, M. (1996). *Children in families: Research and policy.* Psychology Press.

Byng-Hall, J. (2008). The crucial roles of attachment in family therapy. *Journal of Family Therapy, 30*(2), 129–146.

Chase, E., Maxwell, C., Knight, A., & Aggleton, P. (2006). Pregnancy and parent-hood among young people in and leaving care: what are the influencing factors, and what makes a difference in providing support?. *Journal of adolescence, 29*(3), 437–451.

Cheney, K. (2016). 'Blood always finds a way home': AIDS orphanhood and the transformation of kinship, fosterage, and children's circulation strategies in Uganda. In *Childhood, youth and migration* (pp. 245–259). Springer.

Chingono, N. (2021). Half of Zimbabweans fell into extreme poverty during Covid. Retrieved from https://www.theguardian.com/globaldevelopment/2021/jun/21/half-of-zimbabweans-fell-into-extreme-poverty-during-covid. Accessed 5 August, 2021.

Chinyenze, P. (2017). Institutional childcare services in Harare, Zimbabwe: Exploring experiences of managers, caregivers and children. Unpublished doctoral dissertation. University of Witwatersrand, Johannesburg, South Africa.

Christiansen, Ø., Havnen, K. J., Havik, T., & Anderssen, N. (2013). Cautious belonging: Relationships in long-term foster-care. *British Journal of Social Work, 43*(4), 720–738.

Davies, H. (2012). Affinities, seeing and feeling like family: Exploring why children value face-to-face contact. *Childhood, 19*(1), 8–23.

Denton, E. G. D., Musa, G. J., & Hoven, C. (2017). Suicide behaviour among Guyanese orphans: Identification of suicide risk and protective factors in a low- to middle-income country. *Journal of Child & Adolescent Mental Health, 29*(3), 187–195.

Fargas-Malet, M., & McSherry, D. (2021). The emotional nature of birth family relationships for care-experienced and adopted young people: A longitudinal perspective. *Journal of Family Issues, 42*(10), 2263–2288.

Finch, J. (2007). Displaying families. *Sociology, 41*(1), 65–81.

Foster, G. (2000). The capacity of the extended family safety net for orphans in Africa. *Psychology, Health & Medicine, 5*(1), 55–62.

Frimpong-Manso, K. (2014). From walls to homes: Child care reform and deinstitutionalisation in Ghana. *International Journal of Social Welfare, 23*(4), 402–409.

Frimpong-Manso, K., & Bugyei, A. G. (2019). The challenges facing children reunified with their families from an orphanage in Ghana. *Children & Society, 33*(4), 363–376.

Ganong, L., Coleman, M., Fine, M., & Martin, P. (1999). Stepparents' affinity-seeking and affinity-maintaining strategies with stepchildren. *Journal of Family Issues, 20*(3), 299–327.

Gayapersad, A., Ombok, C., Kamanda, A., Tarus, C., Ayuku, D., & Braitstein, P. (2019, December). The production and reproduction of kinship in charitable Children's institutions in Uasin Gishu County, Kenya. *Child & Youth Care Forum, 48*(6), 797–828. Springer US.

Gilbert, K. R. (1996). "We've had the same loss, why don't we have the same grief?" Loss and differential grief in families. *Death Studies, 20*(3), 269–283.

Gilborn, L., Apicella, L., Brakarsh, J., Dube, L., Jemison, K., Kluckow, M., … Snider, L. M. (2006). Orphans and vulnerable youth in Bulawayo, Zimbabwe:

An exploratory study of psychosocial well-being and psychosocial support. Retrieved May 23, 2021, from https://knowledgecommons.popcouncil.org/departments_sbsr-hiv/53/

Gwenzi, G. D. (2019a). Representations of 'family' in residential care: Perspectives from residential care staff in Zimbabwe. *Scottish Journal of Residential Child Care, 18*(2), 1–15.

Hannon, C., Wood, C., & Bazalgette, L. (2010). In loco parentis. Retrieved from https://www.demos.co.uk/files/In_Loco_Parentis_-_web.pdf. Accessed 9 April, 2019.

Hillan, L. (2008). 'What happened to my family?': The place of family in residential care. *Developing Practice: The Child, Youth and Family Work Journal, 20*, 8–13.

Holland, S. (2010). Looked after children and the ethic of care. *British Journal of Social Work, 40*(6), 1664–1680.

Holland, S., & Crowley, A. (2013). Looked-after children and their birth families: Using sociology to explore changing relationships, hidden histories and nomadic childhoods. *Child & Family Social Work, 18*(1), 57–66.

Holland, S., Faulkner, A., & Perez-del-Aguila, R. (2005). Promoting stability and continuity of care for looked after children: a survey and critical review. *Child & Family Social Work, 10*(1), 29–41.

Jardine, C. (2018). Constructing and maintaining family in the context of imprisonment. *The British Journal of Criminology, 58*(1), 114–131.

Juffer, F., IJzendoorn, M. H. V., & Bakermans-Kranenburg, M. J. (2017). Structural neglect in orphanages: Physical growth, cognition, and daily life of young institutionalized children in India. In *Child maltreatment in residential care* (pp. 301–321). Springer.

King, V., & Boyd, L. M. (2016). Factors associated with perceptions of family belonging among adolescents. *Journal of Marriage and Family, 78*(4), 1114–1130.

King, V., Boyd, L. M., & Thorsen, M. L. (2015). Adolescents' perceptions of family belonging in stepfamilies. *Journal of Marriage and Family, 77*(3), 761–774.

Lawrence, E., Jeglic, E. L., Matthews, L. T., & Pepper, C. M. (2006). Gender differences in grief reactions following the death of a parent. *OMEGA—Journal of Death and Dying, 52*(4), 323–337.

Lee, B. R., Cole, A. R., & Munson, M. R. (2016). Navigating family roles and relationships: System youth in the transition years. *Child & Family Social Work, 21*(4), 442–451.

Logan, J. (2013). Contemporary adoptive kinship: A contribution to new kinship studies. *Child & Family Social Work, 18*(1), 35–45.

López, M., & del Valle, J. F. (2015). The waiting children: Pathways (and future) of children in long-term residential care. *The British Journal of Social Work, 45*(2), 457–473.

MacDonald, M. (2017). 'A picture of who we are as a family': Conceptualizing post-adoption contact as practices of family display. *Child & Family Social Work, 22*, 34–43.

Masuka, T., Banda, R. G., Mabvurira, V., & Frank, R. (2012). Preserving the future: Social protection programmes for orphans and vulnerable children (OVC) in Zimbabwe. Centre for Promoting Ideas, USA.

McDowell, E., McLaughlin, M., & Cassidy, T. (2019). Contact with Birth Parents: Hearing the Voice of the Looked After Child: Contact with Birth Parents. *Journal of Social Sciences and Humanities, 5*(3), 194–199.

Mc Mahon, C., & Curtin, C. (2013). The social networks of young people in Ireland with experience of long-term foster care: Some lessons for policy and practice. *Child & Family Social Work, 18*(3), 329–340.

McWey, L. M., & Cui, M. (2021). More contact with biological parents predicts shorter length of time in out of home care and mental health of youth in the child welfare system. *Children and Youth Services Review, 128*, 106164.

Moodley, R., Raniga, T., & Sewpaul, V. (2020). Youth transitioning out of residential care in South Africa: Toward ubuntu and interdependent living. *Emerging Adulthood, 8*(1), 45–53.

Moreno-Manso, J. M., García-Baamonde, M. E., Blázquez-Alonso, M., Guerrero-Barona, E., & Godoy-Merino, M. J. (2018). Empathy and coping strategies in youths subject to protection measures. *Children and Youth Services Review, 93*, 100–107.

Morgan, D. (2011). *Rethinking family practices*. Springer.

Morrow, V. (1998). *Understanding families: Children's perspectives*. National Children's Bureau.

Murray, L., & Barnes, M. (2010). Have families been rethought? Ethic of care, family and 'whole family' approaches. *Social Policy and Society, 9*(4), 533–544. https://doi.org/10.1017/s1474746410000254

Naert, J., Roose, R., Rapp, R. C., & Vanderplasschen, W. (2017). Continuity of care in youth services: A systematic review. *Children and Youth Services Review, 75*, 116–126.

Nyamukapa, C., & Gregson, S. (2005). Extended family's and women's roles in safeguarding orphans' education in AIDS-afflicted rural Zimbabwe. *Social Science & Medicine, 60*(10), 2155–2167.

Paterson, J. E., Field, J., & Pryor, J. (1994). Adolescents' perceptions of their attachment relationships with their mothers, fathers, and friends. *Journal of youth and adolescence, 23*(5), 579–600.

Pauline, B., & Boss, P. (2009). *Ambiguous loss: Learning to live with unresolved grief*. Harvard University Press.

Pinchover, S., & Attar-Schwartz, S. (2018). Is someone there for you? Social support of youth in educational residential care from family, peers and staff. *The British Journal of Social Work, 48*(8), 2195–2214. https://doi.org/10.1093/bjsw/bcx164

Powell, G., Chinake, T., Mudzinge, D., Maambira, W., Mukutiri, S., & UNICEF. (2004). Children in residential care: The Zimbabwean experience. Retrieved August 28, 2018, from https://bettercarenetwork.org/library/the-continuum-of-care/residential-care/children-in-residential-care-the-zimbabwean-experience

Pryor, J., & Rodgers, B. (2001). *Children in changing families: Life after parental separation.* Blackwell Publishing.

Ribbens-McCarthy, J. R. (2012). The powerful relational language of 'family': Togetherness, belonging and personhood. *The Sociological Review, 60*(1), 68–90.

Schofield, G., & Beek, M. (2005). Providing a secure base: Parenting children in long-term foster family care. *Attachment & Human Development, 7*(1), 3–26.

Seltzer, J. A., & Brandreth, Y. (1994). What fathers say about involvement with children after separation. *Journal of Family Issues, 15*(1), 49–77.

Sen, R., & Broadhurst, K. (2011). Contact between children in out-of-home placements and their family and friends networks: A research review. *Child & Family Social Work, 16*(3), 298–309.

Sherr, L., Roberts, K. J., & Gandhi, N. (2017). Child violence experiences in institutionalised/orphanage care. *Psychology, Health & Medicine, 22*, 31–57.

Shklarski, L., Madera, V. P., Bennett, K., & Marcial, K. (2015). Family finding project. *Child Welfare, 94*(6), 67–88.

Smart, C. (2011). Families, secrets and memories. *Sociology, 45*(4), 539–553.

Smyke, A. T., Zeanah, C. H., Fox, N. A., Nelson, C. A., & Guthrie, D. (2010). Placement in foster care enhances quality of attachment among young institutionalized children. *Child Development, 81*(1), 212–223.

Stoilova, M., Roseneil, S., Carter, J., Duncan, S., & Phillips, M. (2017). Constructions, reconstructions and deconstructions of 'family' amongst people who live apart together (LATs). *The British journal of sociology, 68*(1), 78–96.

Soiferman, L. K. (2010). Compare and contrast inductive and deductive research approaches. Online Submission.

Tregeagle, S., Smith, T., & Voigt, L. (2003). Establishing permanency for children-the issues of contact between children in permanent foster care and their birth families. *Developing Practice: The Child, Youth and Family Work Journal,* (6), 57–65.

United Nations General Assembly (2010). United Nations Guidelines for the Alternative Care of Children. Retrieved from https://resourcecentre.savethechildren.net/document/united-nations-guidelines-alternative-care-children/. Accessed 28 September, 2017.

University of Edinburgh (UoE), Childline Zimbabwe and the United Nations Children's Fund (UNICEF) Zimbabwe. (2016). A secondary analysis of childline Zimbabwe data. Harare: UNICEF. Retrieved April 8, 2022, from https://www.unicef.org/zimbabwe/media/336/file/A%20SECONDARY%20ANALYSIS%20OF%20DATA%20FROM%20CHILDLINE%20ZIMBABWE.pdf

Velková, A., & Tureček, P. (2022). Influence of parental death on child mortality and the phenomenon of the stepfamily in western Bohemia in 1708–1834. *The History of the Family, 27*(3), 434–452.

Walker, L. (2019). Careful belonging: Contextualizing alternative orphan care. Retrieved March 18, 2022, from https://archives.northwestu.edu/bitstream/handle/nu/46516/walker_leslie_icd_2019.pdf?sequence=1

Webster, D., Barth, R. P., & Needell, B. (2000). Placement stability for children in out-of-home care: A longitudinal analysis. *Child welfare*, 614–632.

Weeks, J. H., & Heaphy, B. B. & Donovan, C. (2001). *Same Sex Intimacies: Families of Choice and Other Life Experiments.*

Widmer, E. D. (2016). *Family configurations: A structural approach to family diversity.* Routledge.

Williamson, J., & Greenberg, A. (2010). Families, not orphanages. Retrieved December 25, 2014, from https://bettercarenetwork.org/library/particular-threats-to-childrens-care-and-protection/effects-of-institutional-care/families-not-orphanage

Winter, K. (2009). Relationships matter: the problems and prospects for social workers' relationships with young children in care. *Child & Family Social Work, 14*(4), 450–460.

Wood, M., & Selwyn, J. (2017). Looked after children and young people's views on what matters to their subjective well-being. *Adoption & Fostering, 41*(1), 20–34.

Zhou, G. (2012). Understanding the psychosocial well-being of orphans and vulnerable children (OVC): The intersection of research and policy. Honours dissertation. Retrieved May 13, 2021, from https://dukespace.lib.duke.edu/dspace/bitstream/handle/10161/5386/Grace%20Zhou%20FINAL.pdf

Rethinking the Meaning of Family for Adolescents and Youths in Zimbabwe's Child Welfare Institutions

The study findings discussed in the last two parts highlighted the factors that may influence adolescents' and youths' family constructions by definition or membership. The conceptualisation of family was viewed from a Southern African context, where it is common to find child-headed or grandparent-headed households and single-parent families who are also struggling to make ends meet. The comparison with adolescents and youths in families, therefore, did not highlight much difference in family meanings, but it was a useful comparative group. It is common in the developing country context to find cases of child abuse and neglect in families, which may be similar for young people in child welfare institutions. Furthermore, because of the sample of adolescents and youths in families, it was not surprising to find that some of them lacked adequate care and had to rely on support from community members.

This is more common in developing countries than in the Western context (Baldassar et al, 2014). It is common to find orphans and vulnerable children being cared for by someone other than their biological family member, something that is considered inappropriate in the Western context (Baldassar et al, 2014). Developing countries often experience higher levels of poverty and socioeconomic challenges that expose young people to more risk as opposed to those in more developed and more affluent countries. Young people in developing countries in Africa and Asia often end up in institutions due to poverty more than other reasons, compared to those in Western countries, such as Russia, who are mostly in care due to disability or abuse and neglect in Europe (Lumos, 2017).

As a starting point, the challenges faced by young people in child welfare institutions when trying to make sense of their family relationships are brought about by the complexities of their upbringing, which include not only separation from the birth family but also the ensuing experience of being raised by non-kin individuals within the child welfare system. Non-kin caregivers are usually in *loco parentis*, with the state acting as a corporate parent (Bullock et al., 2006). Drawing from their analysis of whether the corporate state can parent effectively, the following four significant differences between living in a child welfare institution and being raised in the birth family are relevant:

- Certain rights and duties become invested in corporate organisations rather than private individuals. Full responsibility is not given to caregivers to parent the children as they please as the study by Gwenzi (2019) found in Zimbabwe. Caregivers must follow the guidelines and procedures of the organisation, including working hours and discipline procedures, which affect the nature of attachments that can be formed with individual children. Parenthood in Zimbabwean society is characterised by personal, comprehensive and continuing commitments to children and is reinforced by mutual emotional attachments between children and their parents.
- When an organisation assumes the care of children, it carries out this role by dividing responsibilities among different groups of people, including birth parents, foster carers, social workers and managers, civil society organisations and probation officers.
- The responsibilities of the organisation are not exact, and the process of care is not as continuous as with families in society. The temporal nature of institutional care impedes the formation of long-term relationships. When youths leave institutional care, they either are reunified with the birth family to continue their relationships based on consanguinity or live independently. Often, family reunification fails due to prolonged periods in separation, which leads to strained relations with the birth family. Young people, in most cases, therefore, always end up relying on unrelated individuals for their care and

support, which, using the contemporary definition of family, could be regarded as "family".

- Young people make new attachments that may supersede, erode or conflict with earlier ones, which creates special tensions for children, carers and the birth family.

It is therefore necessary that in situations where institutional state care cannot be avoided, efforts are made to create a family-like environment in which a child can bond and develop fully even in the context of institutional care. A substitute "family" is to be sought in the instance where the child or young person cannot remain in the care of the biological family (del Valle & Bravo, 2013). There now exists evidence that suggests that institutions of child welfare can become family environments. Scholars have found evidence of the presence of family-like relationships and practices in residential care (see, e.g., Dorrer, McIntosh, Punch & Emond, 2010; Gwenzi, 2020; Johansen & Grabowski, 2021; Kendrick, 2013). In Zimbabwe, while there have been calls to move from dormitory-style institutions to family-based care models, there currently exists no evidence on how this is being implemented. The greater need for institutional care in the context of poverty and rising numbers of children without parental care may make this shift difficult to realise.

In addition, creating a "family-like" environment and being considered "family" by participants in child welfare institutions represent two different ideas. I argue that the creation of a family-like environment means creating an imitation of a "real" family, whereas when adolescents and youths described a non-kin-caregiver as "family", this represented a legitimate category of their social relations and not an imitation. Some of the individuals who were described as "family" were coresident (caregivers, housemates); they shared experiences and significant family practices with the participants and provided love, care and support in the absence of the birth family to the point that participants felt they were a legitimate family.

The line between calling these relationships "family" instead of "family-like" may be subtle, but it is worth acknowledging. The understanding of this nuance will bridge the gap between truly knowing what family means for young people in child welfare institutions. When young people consider an individual as "family" to them, this person is as good as their mother, brother, father or sister. In the absence of the birth family, this is the only family they have. The implication of this is that if practitioners can identify these relationships and nurture them, young people in child welfare institutions can finally develop a sense of belonging, even in the context of care. However, the reality is that these relationships are not considered legitimate, and hence, nothing is done to identify and strengthen them. Adolescents and youths in this study described that no one had ever asked whom they consider to be family. This is similar to findings in a study by Farragher (2019) in Ireland, which also highlighted that it was the first time young people had been asked what family meant to them. This illustrates the neglect of this group of young people in studies about family.

The "family" described by young people in child welfare institutions may be closely linked to the concept of "chosen families" (Weston, 1991), which included both non-kin and nonlegal relationships that were considered "family". Weston (1991) described "families we choose" and how they are formed in multiple configurations in the gay community. In comparison, young people in child welfare institutions, particularly those abandoned and who have lost contact with the biological family, can also "choose" their family based on who is available and supportive in their lives. These chosen families coexist with the "unchosen families" (members of their biological family). Chosen families challenge the long-held heteronormative views of family that privilege marriage, biological parenthood, gender-specific roles and heterosexuality (Powell et al., 2010). Braithwaite et al. (2010, p. 390) also labelled these relationships "voluntary kin", which is also relevant to the constructions made by adolescents and youths in child welfare institutions.

The multiplicity of concepts that could mean family makes it difficult to determine the best definition for the unconventional families described by adolescents and youths in child welfare institutions in Zimbabwe. What further complicates the conceptualisation of family in child welfare institutions is the context in which it is taking place. In a traditionally collectivist society that believes in the notion of "it takes a village to raise a child" and ukama and ubuntu concepts, under a collectivist ideology, we find children and youths living in institutions separated from their families and communities. Even after the decline of the extended family, which was a safety net for orphans and vulnerable children, nuclear families were expected to care for children and youths in need of care. There have been new considerations of kinship care, defined as care by relatives or friends of the family (Mann & Delap, 2020), as a viable option for the care of orphans and vulnerable children in sub-Saharan Africa. There are also examples of kinship care being used in Zimbabwe (see, e.g., Dziro &

Mhlanga, 2018; Muchacha et al., 2016). Relationships based on kinship have continued through ideologies such as community care by individuals from the same village or community who are not blood relatives. Within this context, there is room for a broader conceptualisation of family beyond the nuclear, biolegal definition.

Last, the subject of family is a complex one that may trigger painful memories for adolescents and youths in child welfare institutions. This is due to the circumstances that necessitated their removal and separation from their biological families. Sng (2009, pg. 249) stated that there must be an awareness that, for many children in care, the term "family" may carry some "inescapable negative connotations of abandonment, unpredictability and pain". Thinking through what family means for them is an emotional process, and emotions, which are often negative, may complicate young people's meanings, making them difficult to interpret correctly. Some of the participants in this study refused to engage with the subject of family, leaving the question about what and who is family blank. This was understandable. For those who were able to reflect on their family meanings, it was not a simple task, and this body of work acknowledges and respects that. However emotional the subject may be, it still needs to be explored because family is a critical and often emotional subject for all individuals. Broken and strained relationships with birth families may spur the need for a broader understanding of who can be family and redefine family constellations (Lee, Cole & Munson, 2016).

The conceptual model proposed in this book, therefore, acknowledges the complexity and nuances surrounding young people's constructions of their family meanings.

Describing the Conceptual Model

This conceptual model brings the sociological perspective into a predominantly social work issue, thereby contributing to arguments about the relevance of sociology to social work (Cunningham & Cunningham, 2014; Howland & Crowley, 2013). Holland and Crowley (2013), in particular, argue that the sociology of "family" can enhance the understanding of the lives of young people in institutions. They call for the use of sociological theories related to family and close relationships to understand the lives of care leavers and children currently in substitute living arrangements. Few studies have utilised contemporary approaches in the sociology of family to understand the relational lives of children and young people in out-of-home settings. Recent approaches in the sociology of the family, such as the family practices approach (Morgan, 2011), provide alternative frameworks that move beyond a focus on normative constructions of the nuclear family and stress the historical and spatial fluidity of kin relations. This allowed for an examination of adolescents' and youths' family meanings in a nonnormative living arrangement, the child welfare institution.

Young people living in institutions have been studied for several years within the social work and psychology disciplines, and very few sociological theories have been applied to these studies. More recently, some scholars have begun applying contemporary sociological theories of family in social work, for example, Wissö, Johansson and Höjer (2019); Morris (2012); Jones and Hackett (2011); Kendrick (2013); and Gwenzi (2020).

A combination of theoretical concepts was found useful to explain how adolescents and youths may construct meanings of family while in child welfare institutions. Concepts that helped to explain a) their interactions with multiple individuals, b) the social context and environment with all the dynamics therein, c) participants' attachment patterns based on their childhood experiences and d) the experience of loss during and after separation. The framework was therefore developed from some foundational theories that were found relevant in explaining the social construction of "family", namely, symbolic interactionism, social constructionism, attachment theory and ambiguous loss theory. The overall framework chosen is interpretive social constructionism (ISC), which allows for the consideration of multiple realities and the use of more than one theoretical approach.

The Social Construction of Family

Social constructionists believe in the language of a phenomenon and that knowledge is sustained through social processes (Lit & Shek, 2002). From the study findings, the social construction of family by adolescents and youths can be described as a dynamic process involving the language of family and understood through processes of interaction. Based on this, the study contributes to theory by providing a way to understand the family relationships of young people living in nonnormative child welfare arrangements, in this case, child welfare institutions. Participants described positive relationships that could be described as familial based on the presence of certain qualities and not only blood relations. This implies something that can be explained by more than just social construction theory because it is evidence that not only macro social forces are at play but also young people's own perceptions of their relationships with the individuals they view as family. In this case, the role of symbolic interactionism in explaining how the individual participants interacted with their subjective meanings of "family" is acknowledged.

The interpretive social construction of family acknowledges multiple realities of the family concept, including diverse living arrangements and intimate relationships (Gabb & Silva, 2011). This is where social constructionism interacts with symbolic interactionism, moving beyond the blood relationship and including relationships that are based on interaction and certain practices. The implication is that if the wider society embraces a more diverse definition and understanding of family and relationships for young people in child welfare institutions, there is an opportunity to broaden their social networks.

Kassa (2017) investigated Ethiopian children's definitions of "family" and the type of relationships that count as family. Although this study did not target young people in the child welfare system, it provided a useful basis for the social construction of family membership and the factors that may influence it. Kassa (2017) highlights the importance of understanding the boundaries children draw with regard to their family relationships. She demonstrates how the normative family and "family practices" are shaped by sociocultural, material and spatial contexts by examining the differences between rural- and urban-based children in Ethiopia. Relationships with family were discussed in terms of reciprocity, inclusion, participation and belonging (Kassa, 2016). The same constructivist approach used in the Ethiopian study was applied when formulating the conceptual framework for adolescents and youths in child welfare institutions. An interesting finding in the Ethiopian study was that when birth parents and other close blood relations failed to practise socially meaningful social interactions, the blood relationship ceased to be regarded as important in children's construction of family meanings. When you consider the findings presented in Part V, contact with the birth family contributed to adolescents' and youths' constructions of family in Zimbabwe, and where it was absent, biological family members were not considered as family, and/or unrelated individuals were added to the definition, which supports Kassa's findings in Ethiopia.

Another example that applied a social constructivist approach is *The Family Matters* study in Ireland, which utilised grounded theory to understand how young people with experience of the care system talk about family, how they understand and experience family and how they describe a family relationship. The study found that young people in care do not believe in the idea of a family consisting of only biologically related individuals (Farragher, 2019). Young people in care reported that family is based on the care received from individuals and that family has different meanings for different individuals, which was similar to the findings in Zimbabwe.

Symbolic Interactionism

Symbolic interactionism helps to explain the interactions between young people in institutions and the individuals in their lives. In mutual interactions, family members arrive at an understanding of one another (Hess, Handel & LaRossa 2017). Young people in and out of institutions are exposed to multiple relationships with different individuals during their childhood, which may mean that they are engaged in multiple interactions. However, it has been proven that although there are many interactions, they are of low quality and highly transient. Studies have shown the impact of partial and disruptive relationships with professionals and caregivers in the child welfare system and the unstable nature of institutional placements (see, e.g., Castillo et al., 2012; Herbert, Lanctot & Turcotte, 2016). Due to its focus on meanings and definitions, symbolic interactionism provides a theoretical lens with which to understand what meanings children and care leavers assign to the term "family".

Previously, a symbolic interactionist perspective was used to explore the symbols that can make an individual to be considered part of a "family". Davies (2008), for instance, describes the practice of naming as a factor in how children can identify themselves with their family members through surnames. Winter and Cohen (2005) illustrate how previously looked-after young people can develop identity issues stemming from a lack of knowledge about their origins. Davies (2011) suggests naming as a family practice that structures children's lives and experiences. Some separated young people in institutions may have been abandoned at birth and may not have knowledge of their original family names. While previous studies have shown that a name can be a symbol of belonging to a family for children, this has not been applied to young people in institutions.

Similarly, places have been found to hold symbolic meanings that have implications for the well-being of individuals (Jack, 2015). From a young age, children develop feelings about their surroundings, with specific attachments forming towards people and places that are consistently associated with a sense of security and other positive experiences. A child's secure base is therefore connected to their attachment base and their sense of belonging and identity. This implies that the institutional environment is a key context for adolescents' and youths' constructions of their attachments and relationships, and this was found to be useful for formulating the conceptual model. Figure 7.1 presents the conceptual model for the construction of families by adolescents and youths in child welfare institutions.

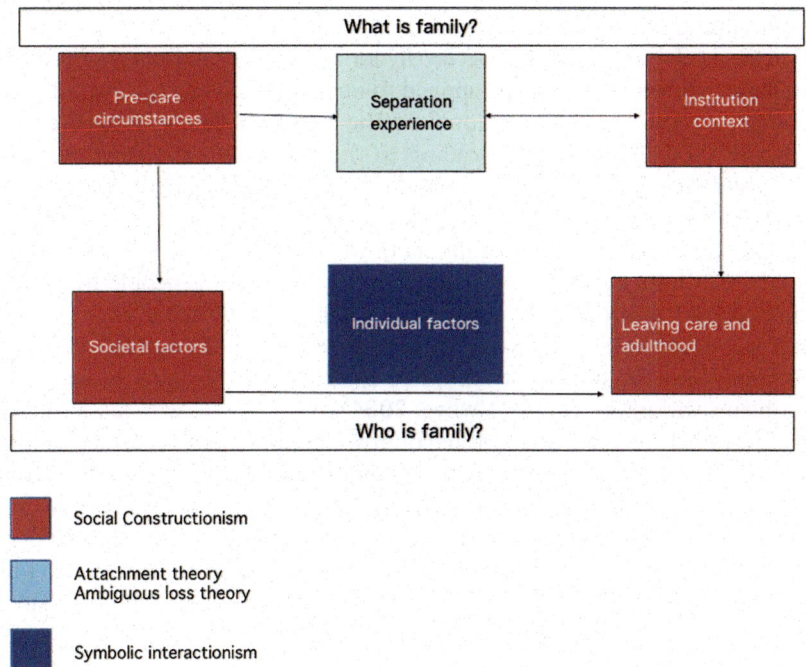

Fig. 7.1 Conceptual model for the meaning of family for institutionalised young people

How to Apply the Model

The model introduced here acknowledges the changes that have taken place in families globally in the last 30 or so years. While families are changing, children and young people are also impacted by those changes. The changing socioeconomic environments also impact families, leading to some children and young people without parental and/or biological family care. For those living in separation from the biological family, it does not mean that family ceases to exist for them. As has been established, the biological family remains a persistent part of their lives, yet very few young people have had a chance to discuss what family means to them while they are in care. Taken-for-granted assumptions of what family means do not apply to those who are living, sometimes for prolonged periods of time, away from the biological family in the care of substitute often non-kin individuals.

This model was designed specifically for adolescents and youths in child welfare institutions but can be applied to understand the family lives of any young person living in separation from the biological family. This entails a consideration of the reasons leading to the separation, the environment the child or young person lives in during separation and the nature of relationships therein, the sociocultural context and the individual characteristics of the young person thinking of what family means for them. The model can be used during social case work with young people living in child welfare institutions to get them talking and thinking about their biological families. Social work in Zimbabwe is silent about the meaning of family and the dominant narrative, even in family therapy focuses on problems within the family (Nwoye, 2004).

In Zimbabwe and most African countries, modern family therapy is not a widespread practice, and when it is practised, it mostly uses Western theories and principles (Nwoye, 2006). However, according to Nwoye (2004), indigenous family therapy has always existed in Africa through the extended family (aunts, uncles, grandparents, etc.). The model can also be applied to family therapy with adolescents and youths in child welfare institutions (e.g., Sng, 2009). Questions about who and what is family can be useful during therapy sessions.

The model emphasises that adolescents and youths in child welfare institutions are influenced by a multiplicity of factors when trying to make sense of what family is. In the model, family is defined based on *family definition* and *family membership*. Factors that influence adolescents' and youths' constructions of family definition begin from their precare circumstances before they are placed in the child welfare institution. The circumstances that led them to be separated from their birth families contribute to their meanings of family, as the study results showed. For instance, neglected children were less likely to include birth family members as their "family" when asked to consider who counts as family. In the institution, several factors influence how young people think about their family relationships, including family contact and length of time in the institution. For instance, the study results showed that a lack of contact negatively influenced family membership. The chances of being counted as a family member were slim for family members who had never contacted the child during their separation and placement in the child welfare institution. It also led to ambiguity in family definitions, with participants either saying they did not have a family or did not know how to respond to the idea of family.

The institutional context also consists of relationships that were described as familial, relationships between adolescents, youths and their caregivers and fellow housemates. These relationships were characterised by love, support, care, and sharing of experiences and moments. Family practices were therefore enacted within the institutional environment and provided adolescents and youths with a sense of family. Individual factors were also considered, such as age and gender, with older youths being more open to broader definitions of family than younger ones and males being more likely to include non-kin individuals as "family". These are also influenced by the societal context all the way until they leave the child welfare institution and transition into adulthood.

Implications for Child Welfare in Zimbabwe

Several recommendations for future child welfare interventions in Zimbabwe come from the study. These are related to both policy and practice of child welfare.

Policies and Interventions to Prevent Child–Family Separation

As a starting point, it is imperative to reduce or prevent the separation of children from their birth families to avoid them relying on institutional care. Once children continue to be placed in institutional care for reasons such as poverty, the emotional and psychological impacts of separation will continue to affect their family relationships. The primary role of child protection social work is to prevent the separation of children from their families (Shangwa & Mathende, 2019). This is in line with international standards set by the United Nations Guidelines for the Alternative Care of Children (United Nations General Assembly [UNGA], 2009). At present, Zimbabwe does not have consistent family-oriented policies designed to promote and strengthen parents' ability to care for their children (SOS Children's Villages, 2014). Family-focused policies guide the creation of programmes such as parenting courses, promote positive parenting, teach conflict resolution skills and provide opportunities for employment and income generation.

Zimbabwe is currently considering the efficacy of family-based and community models of care to discourage the separation of children from communities (Ringson, 2017; Takaza et al., 2013). Although the current child welfare thrust seeks to promote family-based and community-based forms of care, institutional care is still being used in Zimbabwe. The study showed that adolescents and youths also considered non-kin individuals as "family", which brings up the possibility of foster care and adoption for those in need of alternative care. Currently, foster and adoption are not widely adopted in Zimbabwe for cultural reasons, but for vulnerable young people, non-kin individuals who show love, care and support are a viable option that should be considered. Foster care can be based on kinship or non-kinship (Moestue, 2016). The Ministry of Labour, Public Service and Social Welfare may need to sensitise communities around the benefits of foster care and adoption. Social service practitioners can use examples of best practices from neighbouring South Africa and the global world who have used foster care and adoption with some successful outcomes when compared to institutional care (Frost & Mills, 2019). Positive attitudes to well-monitored foster care and domestic adoption can ensure that children who cannot be cared for by their families still grow up in a family environment (UNICEF, 2006).

However, the focus of social policy in this regard should also be on family strengthening to ensure that families are capacitated to care for their own children. In the poverty context that was presented, social assistance programmes, including cash transfers to households that are food-poor or labour constrained, can be useful interventions. Policies should also acknowledge the increasing diversity of family forms in Zimbabwe and should not only focus interventions on households defined according to the traditional definition of family. More inclusive definitions of family are encouraged to provide a wider resource of individuals who can be considered "family" for young people at risk of being separated from their birth families. For instance, the study highlighted the vulnerability of single-parent families or of migrant families who leave social orphans. We need policies that will strengthen the capacity of such family forms to cope with the care of their children. Further, kinship care must be formalised with relevant legislative instruments to guide it. This will ensure that grandparents or other extended family members and friends of the family taking care of vulnerable children and youths may receive monetary support according to various criteria (Moestue, 2016).

Promoting a Better Quality of Care in Child Welfare Institutions

In some cases, the removal of children from their birth families is unavoidable, for instance, when there is clear abuse, severe neglect and exploitation of children. In this case, efforts must be made to ensure better quality of care in alternative care. Efforts should also be made to render family reconstructive services to solve the issues that necessitate children's removal from their birth families. This will make family reunification a possibility. For young people in child welfare institutions, the quality of their care can be improved by reducing placement disruptions and multiple placements. This will promote a sense of permanence and continuity of relationships with their caregivers. The study found that some young people live in child welfare institutions for long periods of over five years. Some of the adolescents had moved once or twice from one institution to the other due to their age. Some institutions only cared for them up to when they are adolescents, and they move to another institution. This affected their relationships with the caregivers they had known since they were younger, and they were now faced with forming new relationships. Some young people may become hesitant to form bonds when they know they have to move again. Hence, ensuring the permanence of institutional placements, especially for those without knowledge of their birth families, is recommended. Permanence can also be created through foster placements, that is, by identifying willing unrelated foster parents within the community who will care for youths for a longer period of time. Foster care has also been identified as a more suitable method of child welfare because young people will live within their communities and are raised within a family environment.

Improving the Knowledge About Youths' Families

Some young people in child welfare institutions do not have knowledge about their birth families. This may be because they were abandoned at birth or because they lost contact with their birth families at a very early stage of their lives. Due to a lack of family tracing services and legislation that mandates residential care facilities to conduct family tracing in Zimbabwe, youths remain in the dark about their birth families. This means that the option of youths being reunified with the birth family when they reach the age of 18 is limited. Youths without family options at the time of their discharge either end up continuing to stay in the child welfare institutions beyond 18 and delay their transitions into adulthood or they end up in the streets. The broader definitions of family found in this study may provide additional social networks of individuals who can provide care for youths leaving child welfare institutions.

More Family Studies in Zimbabwe

The study highlighted the dearth of studies on family in Zimbabwe, particularly studies that examine family meanings, changes and increasing diversity of families. Similar to other countries, Zimbabwe has undergone family changes, and yet, only a handful of studies have documented these changes. Changing family definitions and forms need to be examined in the context of Zimbabwe because they affect the care and welfare of children. In addition, understanding how individuals define "family" is critical for more than research. Social policies and demographic programmes use household data that include family composition, yet we see very few studies conceptualising the meaning of family in Zimbabwe. The danger of this oversight is that we continue relying on traditional definitions of family that no longer apply to the society in which interventions or policies are targeting. Social researchers are also neglecting a critical topic that influences a huge portion of Zimbabwean culture because in Zimbabwe, family is the foundation for most of our existence.

Studies can be conducted across different geographical locations, covering both rural and urban families, family diversity across different tribes and socioeconomic status. This book examined family definitions in child welfare institutions, which is a marginalised topic in family studies. Other nonnormative living arrangements, such as migrant youths and street youths, also need to be explored. Adoption and foster care families also provide a setting to understand the meaning of family in Zimbabwe, although adoption is not a very common practice in this context. Both interpretive and objective research designs on family meanings will contribute greatly to the global literature on family change and diversity. Furthermore, future studies may be comparative, considering different societal contexts to see whether family meanings will have similar or differing characteristics. Cultural differences are bound to make family meanings different; hence, the findings in this study cannot be generalised to all societies.

Final Conclusions

Families are important for everyone, but more so, they are important for children and young people. It has been established that it is critical to consider how children and young people make sense of their family relationships. The social construction of family is not a new subject. Even the notion of a "rethinking" of family is not new, considering the many changes that have taken place in the structure and form of families over the years. Scholars have grappled with what the notion of family means for different groups of people (see, e.g., Turtiainen, Karvonen, & Rahkonen, 2007; Weigel, 2008), and several calls have been made for an ideological shift from traditional, narrower constellations of family to broader ones that speak to the new realities of family. As families have continued to diversify and transform, the debates about what and who counts as family have just intensified. We are still nowhere near reaching a consensus on the meaning of family because of the highly subjective and contextual nature of the subject.

In Southern African countries, particularly Zimbabwe, the notion of family has not been well documented in relation to its subjective meanings. This is in contrast to the more developed countries, which have seen a proliferation of family studies examining families and their meanings for different groups of people. While this book acknowledges the changes that have also taken place in Zimbabwean families and the growing diversity of families in the country, very little is known about what these changes mean for Zimbabwean society. This lack of attention to family meanings is more prominent among vulnerable and marginalised groups in Zimbabwe. This book addressed the gap in the literature on the meaning of family for marginalised young people living in child welfare institutions.

It has been established that cultural and living contexts are key to the social construction of family meanings. Scholars are aware of the inattention that has been given to young people living outside of family care by sociologists (Wildeman & Waldfogel, 2014). In general, child welfare in Zimbabwe is largely understudied, with limited information about actual numbers of children and young people living in institutions. Traditionally, the extended family and community spirit allowed for the care of orphans and vulnerable children and young people to remain in the care of the individuals of the same kin or ancestral lineage. However, the socioeconomic crisis in the country has led to the decline of most of these traditional safety nets for vulnerable young people. However, the lives of young people who end up in substitute care, including child welfare institutions, remain largely undocumented, leaving a huge gap in the academic literature. This neglect is concerning because millions of young people currently live in institutions globally. It is the hope that this book will make a useful contribution to the dearth of literature, particularly in Southern Africa.

This book contributed a conceptual framework for understanding the family lives of adolescents and youths in child welfare institutions that considers their precare circumstances, the separation experience, their time and experiences in the child welfare institution, the social context and individual factors. The conceptual framework allowed for the consideration of different theoretical approaches, namely, social constructionism, symbolic interactionism, ambiguous loss and attachment theories. The separation experience was highlighted in this book as the key context in which family meanings (by *family definition and family membership*) are constructed by adolescents and youths in child welfare institutions. The study sheds light on the complex process of understanding "family" in the institutional context, compounded by the experience of separation from the biological family. This illuminates the potential for social relationships based on everyday interactions in child welfare institutions, which include coresidence and affective practices, not just blood relations. The study also showed how this is further complicated by memories and the emotional copresence of the biological family. However, a new way of understanding institutional relationships that is not overly negative and focused on the effects of institutionalisation but rather on the interactions and family practices was presented.

Family is also dynamic and fluid, not static, especially in the context of biological family separation. The residential care context, which poses a challenge to taken-for-granted assumptions of what it means to be a family, a child or a parent (McIntosh et al., 2011), was used as the setting to show how family meanings can be socially constructed by separated young people. Schofield et al. (2017, p.5) state that "it is only through understanding the young person's sense of their whole childhood, its cumulative and interactive nature that identity construction and the experience of living in and moving on from residential care to independence can be understood". While this study has begun this work, further studies can further explore other processes involved in understanding the family lives of children and young people living in separation from their birth families.

The book highlighted the persistence of the blood relationship despite some negative experiences of institutionalised adolescents and youths, including abandonment and neglect. On the other hand, it also highlighted the increasing diversity of family meanings that previously did not exist in the Zimbabwean context. For many separated young people living in child welfare institutions, this was the first time someone asked them to speak about what family meant for them. Their experiences in the biological family prior to placement in the child welfare institution, their in-care experiences, including the multiple interactions with different individuals in their lives and their own individual characteristics, such as age or perception of their family relationships, all played a part in how they made sense of their family relationships. While the biological family remains the dominant ideal of who and what family is, young people, especially older ones, showed an openness to broader constellations of family. However, it is important to note that, in most cases, extending the family constellation to include non-kin individuals did not replace the biological family but added to it. The implications of this broader, wider network of social relations for young people growing up in alternative care have been noted. Children, adolescents and youths in child welfare institutions and residential care staff need to be made aware that more options can be available in instances when the biological family fails or refuses to provide care and welfare. There are benefits to having a wider social network that builds young people's social capital, including improving their overall well-being, increasing opportunities for employment and building a sense of belonging.

The study also highlighted the agency of adolescents and youths in constructing their own meanings of family based on their personal experiences with the individuals in their lives. For young people coming from a background of social exclusion and marginalisation, this is a positive development. If young people can be provided with more opportunities to voice out their opinions on matters affecting their lives, they will feel more in control of their destinies and future selves. The book also illuminated how the social construction of family goes beyond mere descriptions of what family is to deeper explorations of past and present relationships, the emotions present in those interactions and the way those relationships play out every day. The meaning of family is created through a symbolic and dynamic process that also empowers adolescents and youths to think about who and what family means for them.

This book conclusively motivates a shift in the way society thinks about family as it pertains to adolescents and youths living in nonnormative settings, such as child welfare institutions. Several scholars have called for a need to move away from thinking solely about family in the traditional sense using narrow categories that groups of young people cannot identify with. Broader views about family need to penetrate all sectors of society where families are practised daily, which requires a mindset shift. We simply cannot continue to take it for granted that family means the same thing for every single individual. The results presented in this book have shown that a narrow definition of family is inapplicable for children and youths living outside of biological family care, who are, in most cases, only able to consider non-kin individuals for support, care and affection in the absence of the biological family. It is also inaccurate for some children and young people in the child welfare institution who have been abandoned as infants and grew up knowing only their caregiver as "mother". This is a call to consider rethinking the meaning of family for OVCs in general, including children, adolescents and youths living in child-headed or grandparent-headed households, single-parent families and the children of "small house" parents.

In light of the recent move towards decolonising social work and going back to our traditional models of welfare for children, a broader way of thinking about families will also forge a path towards embracing the principles of *Ukama* and *Ubuntu* in which kinship and community care were practised. If we can think of the broader society as family, we create a sense of oneness that goes beyond blood relations and will serve as a protective factor for orphans and vulnerable children. It is the hope that more scholars in sub-Saharan Africa will heed the call to document more family practices and constructions that support this notion. Together, we can build a better, much safer world where all children and young people can thrive and develop to their fullest potential.

References

Baldassar, L., Kilkey, M., Merla, L., & Wilding, R. (2014). Transnational families. *The Wiley Blackwell companion to the sociology of families*, 155–175.

Braithwaite, D. O., Bach, B. W., Baxter, L. A., DiVerniero, R., Hammonds, J. R., Hosek, A. M., et al. (2010). Constructing family: A typology of voluntary kin. *Journal of Social and Personal Relationships, 27*(3), 388–407.

Bullock, R., Courtney, M. E., Parker, R., Sinclair, I., & Thoburn, J. (2006). Can the corporate state parent? *Adoption & Fostering, 30*(4), 6–19.

Castillo, J. T., Sarver, C. M., Bettmann, J. E., Mortensen, J., & Akuoko, K. (2012). Orphanage caregivers' perceptions: The impact of organizational factors on the provision of services to orphans in the Ashanti region of Ghana. *Journal of Children and Poverty, 18*(2), 141–160.

Cunningham, J., & Cunningham, S. (2014). *Sociology and social work*. Learning Matters.

Davies, H. (2008). Reflexivity in research practice: Informed consent with children at school and at home. *Sociological Research Online, 13*(4), 1–14. https://doi.org/10.5153/sro.1775

Davies, H. (2011). Sharing surnames: Children, family and kinship. *Sociology, 45*(4), 554–569.

Del Valle, J. F., & Bravo, A. (2013). Current trends, figures and challenges in out of home child care: An international comparative analysis. *Psychosocial Intervention, 22*(3), 251–257.

Dorrer, N., McIntosh, I., Punch, S., & Emond, R. (2010). Children and food practices in residential care: Ambivalence in the 'institutional' home. *Children's Geographies, 8*(3), 247–259.

Dziro, C., & Mhlanga, J. (2018). The sustainability of kinship foster care system in Zimbabwe: A study of households caring for orphans and other vulnerable children in Bikita. *African Journal of Social Work, 8*(2), 20–28.

Farragher, R. (2019). Family relationships: A means of fostering stability? Foster, 48. Retrieved September 10, 2019, from https://ifca.ie/wp-content/uploads/2020/12/Foster-7-Full-PDF.pdf#page=50

Frost, N., & Mills, S. (2019). *Understanding residential child care*. Routledge.

Gabb, J., & Silva, E. B. (2011). Introduction to critical concepts: Families, intimacies and personal relationships. *Sociological Research Online, 16*(4), 104–108.

Gwenzi, G. D. (2019). The transition from institutional care to adulthood and independence: A social services professional and institutional caregiver perspective in Harare, Zimbabwe. *Child Care in Practice, 25*(3), 248–262.

Gwenzi, G. D. (2020). Constructing the meaning of "family" in the context of out-of-home care: An exploratory study on residential care leavers in Harare, Zimbabwe. *Emerging Adulthood, 8*(1), 54–63.

Hébert, S. T., Lanctôt, N., & Turcotte, M. (2016). "I didn't want to be moved there": Young women remembering their perceived sense of agency in the context of placement instability. *Children and Youth Services Review, 70,* 229–237.

Hess, R. D., Handel, G., & LaRossa, R. (2017). *Family worlds: A psychosocial approach to family life.* Routledge.

Holland, S., & Crowley, A. (2013). Looked-after children and their birth families: Using sociology to explore changing relationships, hidden histories and nomadic childhoods. *Child & Family Social Work, 18*(1), 57–66.

Jack, G. (2015). 'I may not know who I am, but I know where I am from': The meaning of place in social work with children and families. *Child & Family Social Work, 20*(4), 415–423.

Johansen, L. B., & Grabowski, D. (2021). "Sometimes you just need people around you who understand you": A qualitative study of everyday life at a residential care unit for young people with diabetes. *Social Sciences, 10*(2), 78.

Jones, C., & Hackett, S. (2011). The role of 'family practices' and 'displays of family' in the creation of adoptive kinship. *British Journal of Social Work, 41*(1), 40–56.

Kassa, S. C. (2016). Negotiating intergenerational relationships and social expectations in childhood in rural and urban Ethiopia. *Childhood, 23*(3), 394–409.

Kassa, S. C. (2017). Drawing family boundaries: Children's perspectives on family relationships in rural and urban Ethiopia. *Children & Society, 31*(3), 171–182.

Kendrick, A. (2013). Relations, relationships and relatedness: Residential child care and the family metaphor. *Child & Family Social Work, 18*(1), 77–86.

Lee, B. R., Cole, A. R., & Munson, M. R. (2016). Navigating family roles and relationships: System youth in the transition years. *Child & Family Social Work, 21*(4), 442–451.

Lit, S. W., & Shek, D. T. (2002). Implications of social constructionism to counseling and social work practice. *Asian Journal of Counselling, 9*(1), 105–130.

Lumos. (2017). Children in institutions: The Global Picture. Retrieved April 29, 2019, from https://www.wearelumos.org/resources/children-institutions-global-picture/

Mann, G., & Delap, E. (2020). Kinship care in Sub-Saharan Africa: An asset worth supporting. Retrieved September 20, 2022, from https://www.adamfoghana.com/wordpress/wp-content/uploads/2021/05/kinshipcareinsub-saharanafrica6final12_2020.pdf

Mcintosh, I., Dorrer, N., Punch, S., & Emond, R. (2011). 'I know we can't be a family, but as close as you can get': Displaying families within an institutional context. In *Displaying families* (pp. 175–194). https://doi.org/10.1057/9780230314306_12

Moestue, H. (2016). Data collection on children in alternative care in Eastern Europe and Central Asia. Summary report of TransMonEE 2014 Country Analytical Reports on Children in Alternative Care. Final Draft. Retrieved December 2, 2017, from http://transmonee.org/wp-content/uploads/2016/12/CAR-analysis_synthesis-report_FINAL_draft-30-Sep2.pdf

Morgan, D. (2011). *Rethinking family practices*. Springer.

Morris, K. (2012). Thinking family? The complexities for family engagement in care and protection. *British Journal of Social Work, 42*(5), 906–920.

Muchacha, M., Dziro, C., & Mtetwa, E. (2016). The implications of neoliberalism for the care of orphans in Zimbabwe: Challenges and opportunities for social work practice. *Aotearoa New Zealand Social Work, 28*(2), 84–93.

Nwoye, A. (2004). The shattered microcosm: Imperatives for improved family therapy in Africa in the 21st century. *Contemporary Family Therapy, 26*(2), 143–164.

Nwoye, A. (2006). A narrative approach to child and family therapy in Africa. *Contemporary Family Therapy, 28*(1), 1–23.

Powell, B., Bolzendahl, C., Geist, C., & Carr Stellman, L. (2010). *Counted out: Same-sex relations and Americans' definitions of family*. Russell Sage Foundation.

Ringson, J. (2017). Zunde raMambo as a traditional coping mechanism for the care of orphans and vulnerable children: Evidence from Gutu District, Zimbabwe. *African Journal of Social Work, 7*(2), 52–59.

Schofield, G., Larsson, B., & Ward, E. (2017). Risk, resilience and identity construction in the life narratives of young people leaving residential care. *Child & Family Social Work, 22*(2), 782–791.

Shangwa, I. K., & Mathende, T. L. (2019). Child protection systems in the UK and Zimbabwe: Exporting valuable lessons to Zimbabwe. *Journal of Social Service and Welfare, 1*(1), 49–57.

Sng, R. (2009). Family therapy for kids without families: Working systemically with children and young people in residential care. *Australian and New Zealand Journal of Family Therapy, 30*(4), 247–259.

SOS Children's Villages International. (2014). Assessment Report of the Alternative Care System for Children in Zimbabwe. Retrieved from SOS Zimbabwe Website on February 15, 2017, from https://www.soschildrensvillages.org/getmedia/eeaf524d-4486-4aaf-b786-ea44b3c11295/Zimbabwe-small.pdf

Takaza, S., Nyikahadzoi, K., Chikwaiwa, B. K., Matsika, A. B., Muchinako, G., & Ndlovu, E. (2013). A comparative analysis of impact of alternative care approaches on psychosocial wellbeing of orphans and other vulnerable children (OVC) in Zimbabwe. *Journal of Social Development in Africa, 28*(2), 9.

Turtiainen, P., Karvonen, S., & Rahkonen, O. (2007). All in the family? The structure and meaning of family life among young people. *Journal of Youth Studies*, *10*(4), 477–493.

UNICEF. (2006). Children without parental care. Retrieved December 2, 2017, from https://www.unicef.org/chinese/protection/files/Parental_Care.pdf

Weigel, D. J. (2008). The concept of family: An analysis of laypeople's views of family. *Journal of Family Issues*, *29*(11), 1426–1447.

Weston, K. (1991). *Families we choose*. Columbia University Press.

Wildeman, C., & Waldfogel, J. (2014). Somebody's children or nobody's children? How the sociological perspective could enliven research on foster care. *Annual Review of Sociology*, *40*, 599–618.

Winter, K., & Cohen, O. (2005). Identity issues for looked after children with no knowledge of their origins: Implications for research and practice. *Adoption & Fostering*, *29*(2), 44–52.

Wissö, T., Johansson, H., & Höjer, I. (2019). What is a family? Constructions of family and parenting after a custody transfer from birth parents to foster parents. *Child & Family Social Work*, *24*(1), 9–16.

APPENDIX

QUESTIONNAIRE OPERATIONALISATION (ADOLESCENTS AND YOUTHS IN CHILD WELFARE INSTITUTIONS SAMPLE)

Variables	Sub-items	Values	Questions
Demographics	Age	Continuous	3
	Gender		
	Schooling		
Institutional factors	Age at admission	Continuous	13
	Length of stay	Continuous	
	Reason for admission	Open ended	
	Multiple placements	Yes=1; no=0	
Family relationships	Knowledge about family background	(Likert scale =I know everything 5; I know nothing=1	14
	Sibling relationships	Yes=1; 0=no	
	Contact from family	Yes=1; 0=no	
	Perception on relationships with birth family	Excellent=5; poor=1	
	Location of biological family	Rural=1 Urban=0; I don't know= 2	
	Family symbols, e.g. photographs, memories	Yes=1; no=0 Open ended	
	Family definition	Open ended	
	Family membership	Open ended	
	What is an ideal family?		

(continued)

© The Author(s), under exclusive license to Springer Nature Switzerland AG 2023
G. D. Gwenzi, *Rethinking the Meaning of Family for Adolescents and Youth in Zimbabwe's Child Welfare Institutions*, Palgrave Macmillan Studies in Family and Intimate Life, https://doi.org/10.1007/978-3-031-23375-3

(continued)

Variables	Sub-items	Values	Questions
Other relationships	Who do you go to for support?	Open ended	5
	Visits from non-relatives?	Yes=1; no=0	
Mental health	How often do you worry?	Often=5; never=1	4
	What do you worry about	Open ended	
	What are your future plans?	Open ended	

Index[1]

[1] Note: Page numbers followed by 'n' refer to notes.

Printed by Printforce, United Kingdom